"You can't put it down. This life captured in a book will grip your heart and pull you in. The words on these pages are more than just letters or symbols… they are a revelation of hope."
- Cherish Anderson

"The colorful and energetic language is stunningly original."
- Erik Frampton

"I so enjoyed the book. It was truly an inspiration and so well written. I honestly could not put it down, and really hated to see it end. I guess I have to go back to Patterson & Grisham now…"
- Russell Foster

"What comes out of Hotpants is a deep philosophical message that glows with bold originality and creative style; a thrill ride through the fine things of life."
- Random Amazon Review

"An Incredible Memoir; compelling and uplifting. The writing is lovely, with so many beautiful lines."
- Writer's Digest International Self Published Book Awards

"Emotion jumped out at me from every page. I laughed and cried. The writing was incredible."
- Nejah Tisoncik

"I finished this book in two days, and I will be forever affected by the profound way in which he has verbalized my every thought and emotion. Johnny has an amazing gift in his writing ability. This book should be a movie."
- Mandy Stanford

D1430318

For Mom, Dad, Kristin, and Casey

Hotpants

A dreamless sleep for me is when you drift off, not knowing if you are ever going to wake up, or if they are going to give up on you and leave you to die in your sterile coffin. I woke, however, only to a dry scream among violent struggles against my reality. My irritated eyeballs opened to a soft, white environment filled with a bright void of people. *How long have I been asleep?* More screaming. *Is that me?* My head exploded like a firecracker as the heavy metal pain forced its way out through a puny series of coughs. Tiny war ships paraded through the aching coils of my brain, colliding violently with insane membranes. *Six hours?* Something hurts between my legs. There is a very sharp sting. *Hell?*

Where am I? Why am I here? Whiteness… The people around me had a strange, pulsing glow to them. There were bright machines all around me. It was some sort of deranged hospital scene. My head was locked in a stiff protective helmet and I couldn't move. The helmet felt like lumps of damp papier-mâché. I tried to move my eyes, but some red-hot pain in my sockets blocked them as well. Voices told me about the pain down below: a tube that had been jabbed up into my bladder through the only hole available. "Why?" I cried. *Isn't this the type of thing my friends and I would joke about as being the worst possible means of torture ever to be put upon someone?* Yes! And it was happening to me! At the end of the tube was a small absorbent balloon nested inside my bladder. This balloon was supposed to soak up urine, then send it down the tube and out of my body. The creatures surrounding me said that my bladder was numb, so without the tube, it could explode. I rolled madly, like a blind lion in a foot snare.

Whatever sedated brains I had left began to slow. The intensity was too much, the pressure too heavy. The action slowed and the movements became broken, like a slow shutter speed on a video camera. A small man formed out of the twisted blur in my head. He was lost, and running, and he wore a numbered piece of paper on his jersey like in a marathon. He was looking for something. His head spun, as he seemed to be wandering aimlessly. It surely must have been hard, running, with his head spinning like that.

It was all completely blurred now. A gunshot cracked and the image disappeared. An incredible wave of silence rushed into my world with a jolt, piercing my eardrums and alarming a steady ring. My mind grew sluggish. Gradually the pitch of the ring rose higher - higher than the threshold of hearing and not audible to anyone else, but somehow was inside of me. I tried to remember where I was, or why. *Where to go from here? The only way must have been up, because I'm farther down than ever... I think.*

• • •

Things were beautiful when I was 12. I had amazing friends, a loving family, and a healthy young body. Everything was wonderful. It was like my life was a gift from God or something.

I lived at America's happy pace, and gained average knowledge for my age. Up to that point, my life had all been one road with three simple purposes: fun, food, and love.

I had just begun middle school, which I imagined was the point in life where things weren't a game anymore and that my actions would start to mean something. I thought middle school was the time when real dreams started to form.

I was ready to see what rocket-science, professional sport, or millionaire job was in store for my future.

Sometimes, though, what folks think they're ready for jumps at them from an un-perceived angle. It's like boxing, where a fake right would quickly come from the left. I was more or less ready for a straight jab; the natural joys and dramas of a new teenager's life. However, the jab was actually a devastating kick to the nuts. I had heard about it before on the TV and in movies, but for me, it was, surely, never to happen.

1
Casting Call

September 1997

"Watch it, man."

Interrupting the short peaceful moment I had with my face leaning in my locker, I turned to see a large-stomached kid that had knocked me back inside my tiny space as he budged through the crowd. He had a camouflage shirt on. I started to say something, but he was walking off fast, leaving a strong, sweat-tinged AXE Deodorant smell wafting in his wake.

I shut my red locker and turned toward the stampede of my new classmates swarming their way down the narrow hall of my new middle school. It was my first day at Bode Middle School. *Any of these people could become best friends. Any could be my enemy, bully, or a girl I could fall in love with.* I knew no one, for it was just the first week of the seventh grade.

I joined the flow of the thick crowd, and I could sense a sort of aroma of nascent cliques already starting to form. Materializing jocks, cheerleaders, preps, punks, Trekies, and low-lifes filled the hallways as I looked for my 1st hour Speech and Drama classroom. I kept an eye out for the faces I might recognize from elementary school. I also struggled, like everyone else, to keep a cool and even strut. This was my first impression upon most of these strangers, and I sought to catch a wandering eye checking out my physical coolness. It was a ridiculous phase that I think all seventh graders go through. I thought that it might just make people look at me different when tomorrow comes.

From the river of faces popped up one that I knew. Jackson, one of my most faithful friends all the way from the first grade, reached his white little hand out to mine as if he wanted me to slap it. I gazed down at the pale palm in front of me for a split second.

What may seem like pointless little slaps are really underground reassurances of camaraderie. We were saying that whatever obstacles may come, we will be in this together; that we were stepping in this new water together.

Jackson was a great friend, but he was different. He was a religious kid. Religious people are good people. Jackson never cursed or did anything bad, and he was smart. After the hand-slapping ceremony, he glanced quickly in my direction and issued a small "how's-it-goin" nod and went on.

His religion thing… I guess I never got it. To me, it was just God and God ruled all. I was scared to death of God because I was told that if I didn't believe then I would burn in hell.

Everyone started disappearing into doors along each side of the hallway. The blue painted doors were very tall and intimidating, as if their size depicted the vitality of what was beyond.

Once in the classroom, I made my way to the nearest open chair where I safely began the quest I was ready for; the new phase of my life. This was the beginning of the trail, the swirl in the yellow brick road.

My first day of middle school turned into a week, and the week turned into a week and a half. Everything was going well. I already had a good idea of my life for the next six years until I graduated; popularity, girlfriends, and I was destined to be one of the cool kids.

• • •

The ripping headaches attacked me regularly since the sixth grade. It was the feeling of a fever, how the pain was just all over my head, aching with every thought. It felt as if whenever I would move, the soft brain inside would slosh around and bang up against my skull. I would keep my head down and face straight to hide any pain, yet I found it most difficult to keep my eyebrows from crinkling.

Though I struggled to hide the pain from my growing social life, I always exaggerated it to my parents thinking it would create sympathy and have them kiss it and make it better or something. Mom would kiss my head, then tell me how starting a new level in school, especially middle school, could be stressful and cause headaches. She told me that Tylenol would help - a practical cover-up for the pain, but the little red and white universal pills failed to shield the rapid beat in my head. She then thought it must have just been "all in my head".

Mom is Jane Cathcart. Her cozy white face and dark eyes that I depend on so much are symbols of unfailing love that would always be there for me. She is the greatest mom in all the world.

Her theory made sense; she told me with her sweet and gentle voice that I could overcome the headaches if I just tried not to worry about the new school. *But I'm not worried at all!? I am having the time of my life at school!* Maybe there was a different reason my head was hurting. I began to rethink how many times I had clumsily run into doors throughout my life.

However, Dad, being a doctor, suggested that I was getting migraines. His name is Rocky, not like Balboa, but like the real-life boxer Rocky Marciano. When Dad was born in Texas, his scrunched face resembled that of my Grandpa's favorite boxer after a fight. The name "Rocky" was bestowed upon him by his dad David, a boxer himself. Dad was raised in Texas and eventually moved to the Midwest to study medicine and would ultimately settle with Mom in St. Joseph, Missouri. At an even six feet, he also has blue eyes and a light but strong build. If I had to compare his physical appearance to anyone, I'd say Kevin Costner, JFK, and Jack Nicholson all melded into one. Dad, being a doctor, asked me specific questions as to where my head hurt, when, and how. It seems that if doctors know the answer to those questions, then they can magically make it all right. I told him about the double-vision that had come on within the past few weeks. Upon hearing this, he said immediately, "We'd better send you for an MRI and to see a neurologist."

My two older sisters, Kristin and Casey, didn't really bother me with advice about my head. They were just concerned. I was their little brother who they were supposed to protect and make sure I made it through youth without getting into too much trouble. Kristin had short blond hair. She had been a dancer since she was young. By the time I was 12, she was in her first year of the dance program at Kansas University. Casey was just starting her senior year at Central High School. They both handled their big sister jobs well.

Anyway, to end all of the educated wondering about my sore head, it was time to have it looked at. Dad naturally had several doctor acquaintances and a suggestion for the best person to see. He sent me to neurosurgeon Dr. Patricio Mujica. Dr. Mujica was supposedly the top expert of this kind within the area.

• • •

The third Wednesday at Bode Middle School passed slowly by. I stared down that big black and white clock on the walls until the bell rang.

I was thinking about my doctor visit on the way home, and was expecting to hear more lame explanations for my headaches, "It's all in your head!" "Just get more sleep." "You are probably just stressed out." No matter what the diagnosis, Dr. Mujica was expecting my arrival at precisely 5:00.

Mom, Dad, and I pulled up to a dark red office building in the middle of the hospital village that sits on the edge of St. Joseph. The hospital is enormous, like a university campus. I wouldn't be surprised if there was a separate zip code for our hospital.

We stepped out of our car together and silently walked up the long driveway to tall glass doors that stood before us like daunting castle gates. I read the powerful letters on the sign above them: 'Patricio Mujica, MD.' Based on the size of his name, I could tell that this man was wise and important.

The heavy doors led us into an oversized room, with a stiff pond of light blue carpet. Rows of boring chairs with blue upholstery lined the dull blue walls that enclosed the graying and wrinkling people waiting in them.

Massive piles of prehistoric magazines heaped themselves on each sterilized table that sat beside every six or so chairs. After wandering around we found a good spot in the corner next to a small television hanging from the ceiling.

After an hour or so past my scheduled appointment time, I woke from my lost gaze to hear my name called from the open door to the unknown area beyond. A large lady with a curly afro escorted us into a smaller room where I waited yet another half hour for the doctor to come in. This square room was mostly white. It contained a single high, white bed lined with white tissue paper. The skinny pillow at the end was also lined with tissue paper. I hopped on the stiff mattress and began playing with the doctor tools attached to the wall behind me. Dad, being a doctor, explained to me what each thing did. I noticed what was obviously some sort of blood pressure testing thing

8

standing next to me and looked it over with curiosity. Then I picked up the rubber hammer lying on the table next to me and began drumming with it. After several edgy minutes, the door unexpectedly creaked open with a swift gust of cold air, followed by the great neurosurgeon Dr. Pat Mujica. He stood short and penguin like with a well-starched shirt, toffee colored skin, and friendly eyes. He greeted each one of us with a quick handshake.

Mujica turned to me with a funny little smile and began asking me the questions I figured he would ask. "Where does it hurt, how long has it hurt…" and such. I couldn't say where the pain was coming from exactly, I just told him it was "about right here," (circling my hand around my entire head). After a series of "Mmmmms," he comically waddled away, writing things on a clipboard, and a few minutes later, a nurse walked in with a small set of polished tools. There was a needle, a long skinny tube, and some frosty-looking sterilizing materials. Instantly, my heart leapt to my throat. I knew exactly what sorcery she intended to practice on me. I rudely whispered a quick complaint to Dad about the mad nurse with the needle. She must have overheard, because I could of sworn she whispered an evil chortle "MUUHAHAH!!!" and almost mockingly assured me there would be no pain, only a little sting…

I sat tightly in my little spot on the bed and shivered fear. The nurse tried to explain to me that she had to hook a small tube up to a vein in my arm so she could flow medicine through my body. Actually the IV was to pump some contrast fluid into me. Contrast is a sort of juice that circulates throughout the body and glows, revealing my insides to the MRI machine. The nurse instructed me to "flex your big muscles" so she could view my selection of veins. I clenched my fist tight. She found a nice vein and began to wipe the spot where she was going to stick the needle in with a gold paste. She then knotted a rubber band tightly around my bicep, pinching off the blood flow. She angled the steel needle towards my arm and slowly moved in, as if she wanted to build tension; keep me on the edge of my seat. She started a countdown from three. I began to feel Mom's warm grip squeeze tight around my free hand. The seconds were almost up. She was really close now…

After the crying and rolling of veins, the large nurse taped the pierced site up so the needle could not budge. She tied a board around the bottom of my arm in order to prevent me from bending it. Then, to top off the lovely bundle of bandages around my IV, she put a plastic covering over it.

A few moments passed as I recovered from the needle event. Then a different woman entered. She told Mom and Dad to go back to the waiting room, and had me follow her down a skinnier hall into a dark and noisy room that was centered around a giant machine with a large tube through the middle. The machine reminded me of the play place at McDonalds. The tube in the middle was just big enough for a small child to climb through, and was surrounded by all sorts of machinery and cranks and robotic things. The room was chilly, and small goose bumps began to pop up all down my arms and legs as I walked in. A technician emerged from behind a curtain, and started explaining what the machine was, and she told me not to worry just like the previous nurse.

The tube was for people to lie in while the machine took pictures of the soft tissue in their guts. It was an MRI (Magnetic Resonance Imaging) scanner. The woman told me to take off my jeans and any metal I might have been wearing before I came close to the machine. She said that metal could not come near it. To demonstrate her point, she walked to it and held up a metal chain. Magically, the heavy chain instantly levitated and seized at a 90 degree angle, pointing directly at the MRI scanner. It looked as if the machine was yanking the chain through the cold air. The technician hid back behind the curtain while I changed into the hospital pants and gown she gave me. I carefully approached the uncharted mechanism and twisted my half-naked body into the tube. The technician, dressed in what looked like blue pajamas, came to me and tucked a warm blanket around my body like a baby, right up to my chin. Every part of my body was either taped or tucked so that I could not move. The lady strapped big headphones around my ears so I could enjoy the radio while my guts were being photographed.

After everything was double-checked and set, the lady slowly rolled me back deep into the giant tube. There was an airy sound inside, as if hundreds of big fans were blowing inside of a gymnasium. Once in the tube, I waited for about five minutes for something to happen.

Suddenly, a pounding jolt shrilly interrupted the radio and all pleasant sound there ever was. It was like a locomotive trying to accelerate from zero. A thunderous sequence of strange mechanical sounds followed. It made the most bizarre and deafening sounds as it worked. The sounds of this machine can only be described accurately to one who has been in the tube; it's the craziest assortment of ZZZEEEEEEPS, BOPPPS, and BIIIIPPPIITTTZZZXX known to humankind. The chain of torturous racket lasted for nearly 20 minutes and finally came to an abrupt halt. I tried my hardest to remain as still as I could like everyone told me. However, it was difficult to lay perfectly flat and still for that long under such conditions. The whole time, my body wanted to swallow, cough, or itch at something, but it couldn't. Silence... Minutes passed.

Just as unexpected as the first, another noise kicked in: different, but with the same deafening and insane quality. The strange noises pounded their way through my ears. My brain compensated, and it wasn't until the nonsense seemed to settle into a monotonous hum that I began to drift off to an uncomfortable sleep. After another hour or so of these cycles, I woke as I was being pulled out of the tube. I gradually began to rise as the world around went from fuzzy to dizzy. I recognized the large nurse from earlier when she rushed in and started yanking off the bandages around my IV. Tightly pressing a cloth over the site of the needle inside of me, she yanked it away and then put strong pressure on my arm. The pain brought with the

11

needle's departure was almost worse than the pain of the needle going in. I held the cloth firm against the hole in my arm as the sting took its time to ease. She slapped a cute trademark Band-Aid on my arm and exclaimed that I was "all ready to go!" I got up and walked woozily around the room with my new Looney Tunes bandage on. I felt like a drunk in a mental hospital. I couldn't walk straight or even hear right. I was guided around to my clothes on the desk nearby and put them on with great difficulty. I found my parents sleeping in blue chairs in the hall outside. It was time to go. We would find out the results of my MRI the next day.

• • •

It was the day following my MRI, and I had recently joined the Bode Cross-Country Team. It had only been a few days of practice, and I thought I liked it. The friends were good and the athletic stuff was cool, but my headaches were so bad, they interfered with running. It only made my sore brain bang around in my hard skull even harder. I didn't even make it through practice that day.

I came home about 5:00 in the evening and treated myself to some television and cold cereal: the best food in the world. Adjacent to a long wooden hallway through the giant brick house we lived in, were several rooms on either side. One of them was our little TV room, complete with a comfy red love seat and a 24-inch TV. The room could be closed off to make the perfect private hideaway. I didn't have the doors closed most of the time however, because it almost made me feel claustrophobic. I was curled up in the cushions of the love seat busily watching an evening episode of *Doug* on *Nickelodeon*, when I heard the floor creaking. It sounded like an unfortunate overweight person trying to sneak a snack at night but the floor had

12

given them away. It was young Mr. Mischief, the family cat.

By the time I was twelve, Mr. Mischief had pawed upon this earth for nearly 6 years. My sisters picked him from the pet store because of his unique appearance. He was much more attractive than the other cats - in fact, the most attractive cat I had ever seen. I remember seeing him in the cage at the pet store. He just didn't look right sitting in the cages next to all of the other kittens. *"I'm just so much better than these other cats... What am I doing here anyway?"* His facial expression only complemented the size of his body. His face was wise with brownish gray stripes throughout.

Mr. Mischief came into the little TV room to join me. I was always entertained by watching him jump up on the couch. At first glance, you wouldn't think he could make the two-and-a-half-foot leap, but Mr. Mischief never failed to amaze people. One of my favorite things to do with him (that you could never do with normal cats) was to rest my head on his stomach like a pillow. My head would rise up and down with his breathing. Mr. Mischief never seemed to mind. I'm sure he enjoyed the company.

It was nearing 6:00 when Dad returned home from work at his hometown business, the Med Clinic. I identified the strident footsteps on the wooden floor of the foyer, that echoed throughout our big old house. The ceilings were so tall and the rooms were so spacious that almost any sound came off as thunder.

He walked by the TV room and didn't notice me, I spied the stressed look in his face. I could see the gloom in his tired eyes. *Hard day at the clinic...*

Mom was humming merrily and preparing a warm meal for the evening. Mom must have noticed his gloom as well, because the humming ceased as my dad entered.

Mr. Mischief and I continued to watch *Doug* in the TV room. A few moments of silence from the kitchen sent an uncomfortable message my way. Worry and uneasiness began to fog the kitchen and fill the hallway, wafting through the open door of the TV room.

The vents spewed a cold draft. *Doug* continued. I didn't find myself laughing at Skeeter Valentine or Mr. Dink - neither did Mr. Mischief. After a while, I walked out to find my parents.

The kitchen was empty, except for a pot of noodles steaming innocently on the stove that had just been turned off.

It was always a difficult task to find someone in my house. There were five maze-like floors stacked on top of each other. Each comprised of dark narrow hallways that seemed to lead in circles. I didn't like walking through it alone. I always sensed that the spirits which enigmatically inhabited the great mansion were peeking at me from behind corners.

After an unsuccessful hunt inside, I navigated down the creaky staircase and went outside to the porch. I found both of them sitting on the steps leading to the main entrance. Slowly opening the front door, I received a glance from Dad. There was a quiet and chilly breeze running through his hair, making him look like a legendary warrior who had just found his horse slain with his own sword. He nodded me over, with the same pale frown from earlier. Silence.

The uneasy feeling from school began to come up towards my watering eyes. *Why am I about to cry? Why are they already crying?* The silence continued as I sat on the steps. He started to say something but stumbled. " John, the…" a deep breath, "The Doctor looked at your MRI scans." "Oh..?" "There's a tumor," he said. "He found a brain tumor."

Although I didn't understand what a brain tumor was, I noticed more of the most tragic-looking tears slip down both my parents' frightened faces. I joined. Tears fell for a while. I didn't know what else to do but cry with them. I don't think they knew what to do either. *Am I about to die or something? What does a tumor mean?* As my parents held me in their arms and their tears wetted the top of my head, I looked out into the night for answers - the quiet and still night, wise like Mr. Mischief's eyes. The humid sky had just started to shed tears of light rain. Trees around our yard slumped over low, as if they knew what was going on. My parents were so sad, they looked as if they were going to die along with me. The night was heavy, unbearably heavy. *A brain tumor... What is it...?*

. . .

The tumor was at the base of my brain in the rear, close behind my right ear. It was growing rapidly, squashing my brain away and causing my headaches. Surgery had to remove it immediately or else Dr. Mujica said the tumor would kill me within days. The next day was a Friday, and for all I knew it would be my last. I would go to school one last time, and right after, to the hospital in order to prepare for surgery early the next morning.

I kept quiet at school the next day. My nervous attitude had attracted little attention. The bell rang, and I didn't get to enjoy a final cross-country practice. Though I left without saying a word, somehow news of my misfortune not only broke its way through walls and traveled around school, but around town as well - all in just that one day. There was quite an unexpected crowd in the waiting room the next morning.

It was really just like a hotel. I arrived at the hospital with Mom and Dad Friday evening, we checked in at the main desk and took the elevator to the fourth floor. I stepped

15

inside the elevator and watched the doors automatically slide shut to lock us in. I examined the cold, bland walls, and thought about how this was life for some people… a whole community of people that lived and worked at the hospital.

A nurse was watching me stare into space and she interrupted my thoughts. I realized that the doors had opened and we had stepped out onto the fourth floor already. The nurse's face was straight and calm as if she did this 100 times a day. She was nicely dressed in her typical nurse uniform, complete with the light blue baggy pants, and a white cotton over-shirt sprinkled with cartoon characters and flowers. She escorted us to our room.

There were endless corridors on either side with rows of room numbers on each wall fading into the great distance of the long hallway she led us down. Every ten or so rooms there was a small workstation for all of the nurses working nearby rooms. The nurses at each station looked up and smiled at me as I passed, almost as if they'd been expecting me.

Passing the rooms, I could see inside through a small window in each door. A single patient occupied each and every room, sometimes accompanied by a family member or two. Most of them were very old people who were alone and staring at the ceiling. Some were lying in a high bed eating what looked like a TV dinner and staring up at a TV in the corner. A few of the patients noticed me through their doors and briefly met my eyes, silently passing off a strange look of pity, warning, and companionship all at once. The wide-eyed confusion and disbelief on my face, but at the same time regret, and a short painful memory must have compelled them to award me the look every new patient probably gets from such veterans.

The nurse leading me stopped at a door among the lost chambers of the hallway after about two long minutes of walking. The door swung open, and my eyes first laid sight upon this home away from home: my palace, my hospital room. I sucked in the cool, sterile air and studied the room's ghostly aura. I stepped inside. There was a small TV on the ceiling in the corner. A clean white bed sat in the middle of the room to greet me with a dry emptiness, sort of like Lurch the butler. Next to it were some uncomfortable-looking recliners and a door that led to a tiny bathroom. My parents dropped the bags as we were to "make ourselves at home for the night."

After exploring the electronic bed that I could move up or down with a remote, I unpacked my bag. Out came my CD Walkman, (There were no musical smart phones back then. The best technology available was the anti-skip setting), a *Goosebumps* book, and a box of Cheezits.

After settling in, I looked around to find a few interesting tools behind my head. They looked like the ones I saw in Dr. Mujica's office. I recognized the eye and the ear tools, and the blood pressure thing next to it. I went down the line and started to notice more stuff. There was a plastic bag hanging on the end of a pole filled with what looked like water. A tangled tube hung from it that wasn't attached to anything. My eyes then came to the counter next to the pole. On it, lay some small needles with wings that looked like butterflies. I started to get a little frightened again. Coming out from it was a little tube about the same size as the one stuck in me the other day. Alongside the array of needles and tubes sat a box of sterile alcohol wipes, other skin cleaners, and some Band-aids. I also noticed a giant rubber band just like the one from the other day.

Someone nudged my shoulder. It was a guy nurse. He reached out his hand to me, "Hey big guy, I'm Mike. I'll be your nurse for the night. Cool?"

"I'm John, and I'll be your patient."

"He he" He giggled. "Of course. It's nice to meet you. Here, you just make yourself at home while I check your vital signs. Then, I'll hook up your IV and you'll be all set for the night. Also, in about thirty minutes, I'll bring you your dinner. How's that sound?"

"Wonderful," I said.

He took the blood pressure machine I was just looking at and wrapped it around my arm. He then popped a thermometer in my mouth. The pouch around my arm began to fill up with air, and eventually squeezed so tight that it cut off my circulation. After a second or two, the blood from my shoulder burst through under the pressure and quickly filled the rest of the veins in my forearm. Then another pumped through, and another. It was weird and uncomfortable. This went on for about six seconds to the point where I almost couldn't stand it any more. Then the pouch let out the air and eased up on my arm.

"Feels pretty tight, don't it?" Mike said. "Well, you'll get the hang of it very soon. I promise." He seemed to emphasize the word "very."

After my thermometer beeped and he popped it out, he picked up the needle that looked like it had two wings coming out of it. He called it "the butterfly needle," which sounded somewhat sinister. He wiped my arm down with the gold skin cleaning stuff, then he aimed the butterfly at my arm. First, he tried to poke one arm, and the needle wouldn't stick in my vein; it would roll off of it inside my arm, like trying to stab a thin metal pole with a ballpoint pen, or a grape with a fork. He pulled the needle in and out and in and out trying to stab my vein but it didn't work. It was like a bad fishing day. So he tried digging in the other arm a few times and finally pierced a vein. The site of the IV was taped and boarded up like before. The bag filled with the fluid actually contained saltwater that would pump into me all night in order to keep my IV "open." All night I struggled to drift into any type of sleep, but it was most impossible. Everything from the IV hurt. It was hard to sleep with because I had to keep my aching arm perfectly straight the whole time to keep the needle from moving out of place. However, the physical pain was only half of what kept me from my sleep. *Tomorrow, I am going to have brain surgery.* It sounded too sick to make sense. I've seen it on the Discovery Channel before where they would attach humongous entanglements of wires and machines to a person's head, then drill it open with what looked like a Craftsman power drill, and poke at it with long shiny objects.

• • •

Well, the morning inevitably came. A nurse walked in the room to wake me at about 5:30 in the morning. I wasn't very alert at that time, and all I remember was being strolled in my mobile bed down the big hallway. The woman was taking me to surgery, to some feared end of the hospital. My family was following. Mom was holding on to my hand tight enough to upset the nurse who had to present me to the surgeons in perfect condition. As I became more alert, I could feel her nervousness add to mine through the vibration of her hand.

 On the way, I gathered looks from various people doing some early morning wandering around the hospital. Everyone looked at me with the same concerned and sympathetic frowns. They knew that I was about to go through something bad, like passing a fellow inmate on their way to the chair. They wanted to help me, but at the same time they really didn't want to get involved with whatever poor situation led me to that bed destined for the sterile area, or with what horrors that may be waiting for me beyond.

We reached a big door that read "SURGERY," and the first big blue waiting room was behind it. There were a few people already in there for various reasons. The nurse rolled me through the door at the other end to a small

19

hallway with some more doors. The tension rose with each door.

At the end of the way a huge door read "STERILE," a couple others "EXAM ROOM," a larger one read "RECOVERY." First, the nurse took me into one of the exam rooms to check my vital signs. She then rolled me back out to my family who were now sitting in a smaller waiting area next to the "STERILE" room.

It was time for me to head off alone. My family gave their last expressions of love and encouragement, then had to stand still and hand the life of their son over to Dr. Mujica, a group of assistants dressed in blue pajamas, and some finely-sharpened blades. Mom freed my hands for the last time and now could only watch her son being rolled off into a completely unpredictable future. It was a Hollywood worthy dramatic scene. I sat up on my bed and looked back at Mom. She tried to hold them back so I wouldn't be scared, but tears reluctantly ran down her face. Being rolled away on the bed into the forbidden area was like falling off of a cliff to the judgment at the bottom all in slow motion. I felt a little like the poor raccoon in Ace Ventura. I was reaching out a hand to my family that I could never touch, but drift farther and farther away from until there was not even eye contact, just faith.

As I turned back toward the direction I was headed, the doors were already opening. Trembling as I was wheeled through the doors, I had the strange sense that I was crossing a threshold into another world, that nothing would ever be the same after this point.

Instantly everything got brighter. The room was completely white. Everyone moved quickly now. The nurses and doctors seemed to be rushing around frantically. I could feel my pulse quickening as my eyes jolted from one direction to the next. They started grabbing and pushing at me. "OK JOHN, I WANT YOU TO JUST SCOOT YOURSELF ONTO THIS OTHER BED HERE." The commands seemed too loud and too fast. Faces appeared all over, gathering around me as I lay like I'd just lost a schoolyard fight and everyone was looking down at me.

Someone put this breathing thing on me, covering my nose and mouth. Strange air was forced into me. It tasted like a sterile, cold, minty piece of rubber... but... in my nose. At the same time, some lady to my left was injecting a white goopy Elmer's Glue like liquid into my IV tube. It was the anesthesia that was supposed to put me to sleep. My wide eyes followed the goop as it traveled slowly down the tube, closer and closer to my arm. When it finally hit my forearm, I felt a series of stings as it burned through the veins in my arm like Drano through a clogged pipe. As it crept up my arm into my shoulder, my world began to slow, and I could have sworn I heard the sounds of the ocean or a series of rushing glitches in the ambience, like a thousand nails hitting the floor as everything grew white.

• • •

Mom and Dad told me the first ones to show up were Grandpa and Grandma Gray, Mom's parents; a classic looking set of grandparents: old, wrinkly and cute.

One of the deacons from our church was there, and some other members came to pray. Some of my dear old teachers from elementary school also showed up. The room filled up fast.

Prashak, a best friend of mine since the first grade was there. As dorky as he acted sometimes, I stuck by him all through childhood. I shared things with him I'd never share with anyone else. Being so young, we didn't understand the thought of one of us getting seriously hurt, let alone dying. He came early that morning with his parents, who cared for me like a second son. Prashak cried and cried, unable to handle the weight of the morning.

Later that morning, Taylor, my friend from across the street, came in with his parents. Taylor and I both dreamed of the future

21

when we would play in the NBA. I wondered if he still thought I was going to play with him in the pros after this. Although one of the toughest 12-year-olds I knew, tears dripped from his eyes as well.

In addition to my friends, Mom and Dad were also responsible for a whole crowd that wandered in and out. Friends of my sisters, and of my grandparents; in and out. Dad's doctor friends checked in and out. People who ever had any sort of acquaintance with my family or me, and some people who never had any acquaintance with my family, but had acquaintances with people who had acquaintances with my family; in and out.

There was an average of about 40 people in the waiting room during all times of the morning. They must have talked about all sorts of stuff. It was more or less a small town meeting.

"Dr. Cathcart's son is having brain surgery," the adults would say. "John's having part of his brain taken out," my friends would say. Everyone had to come see what was going down with my brain.

One guy, however, did not merely cycle through. Mom told me that he came about an hour into my surgery and stayed the entire time. He didn't speak to anyone. He wore black combat boots, camouflage pants, and a tight black shirt that his large stomach poked out of a little. His eyes were closed most of the time. Near the end of my surgery, he got up to mumble something to himself, and quickly walk out of the room.

It was probably frustrating for my family to feel like they had to thank and entertain every guest that showed, even if they had no idea who they were, like the guy with the camouflage. It was like when you have something big going on and everyone wants to be a part of it, but you are a little bit selfish and want to experience it on your own. But I believe it was the friends and family that kept them from falling apart completely.

It hurts awfully to kndow that Dad was crying. He has always been my real best friend. My family raised me to become something. Now it seemed like life was ending. There was nothing they could do but wait and hope, or maybe pray, as if that were going to help.

2
Gates and Flames

Four Months Earlier

The bright and colorful April morning light pried open my eyelids. After a series of yawns, I smiled as I sucked in the crisp, fresh air of the day. The sixth grade was going to end soon, and it was one of the last Saturdays of the school year. The big screen TV was in front of me. I had slept comfortably late down in the big basement after playing video games all night. Dad had just bought me the newest and coolest Nintendo system, the *Nintendo 64*. *Mario 64* was one of the first games to come out for it. All night I led the little Italian plumber through this 3D world of unimaginable situations and characters that would ultimately lead to the rescue of the Princess Toadstool.

I lived like a king during the mornings. I sat at my big breakfast table up in the kitchen and watched my lovely mom pour me a satisfying bowl of my favorite cereal. It has always been my favorite food. Fruity Pebbles, Cinnamon Toast Crunch, Cocoa Puffs… goodness. I ate my cereal as if experiencing Heaven with each and every bite.

I would always fill the bowl with more milk than I needed, and this is because I kept a cereal/milk ration of about 1/3 in each spoonful. When the bite entered my mouth, my teeth grabbed and held the cereals in place firmly at the front of my mouth but not with so much pressure as to crunch yet. With my amazing sucking action, I'd bring in the milk from the spoon, filtering it through the cereals and down my throat. Then I chewed the milk saturated cereals, completing the perfect two-gulped bite. During the sacred consumption, I watched cartoons. A nice action/drama episode of *Sonic The Hedgehog* or *Mighty Max* completed my royal morning.

That evening we were supposed to go to this play that was touring around to different churches and was playing at a local Baptist church that night, "Heaven's Gates and Hell's Flames."

I've never been to a real play outside of my elementary school performances. I was a little excited, but since it was at a church it meant that I had to dress up in my "nice" clothes.

I was always upset at how I looked when Mom made me tuck in my shirt. I had to pull the khaki pants from my closet and wear a white dress shirt that was too big. Then I put on my cowboy boots which were the only dressy pair of shoes I would wear.

Everything about my image would change when it appeared in a mirror. My ears stuck out more along with my freckles, and my face grew smaller and dorkier in the mirror. My thin, blonde chili-bowl was more defined with all of the hairs out of place. My blue eyes looked awkward in the middle of the brown freckles on my face. My skin was like a brown-spotted birddog. In the mirror, I was too short as well. One day though, I knew I would grow up and everything about my physical appearance would form together and look right, like Dad. He was six feet tall and carried a nice set of well-proportioned features. I knew that when I grew up, I was going to be at least his size.

School ended that day and we were on our way to Westhill Baptist Church where the play was showing. Westhill was about the size of a 400 meter track. The lot was packed with cars and minivans.

As we walked through the lot up to the church, Mom and Dad were ahead, Kristin and Casey were holding hands and giggling together at their jokes, and I lagged behind by myself as the odd number in the family, daydreaming at the daunting steeple and the large, heavy doors of the church as if it were an old castle.

We walked in and immediately to our right stood a small bald man in a suit jacket behind a dark old desk. My parents paid the old man for our tickets. He handed them over very carefully. He must have either been at that age where you just do everything with extreme slowness, or he might have been handing us something of unpredictable worth that tugged at his conscience as to whether or not he should be handing us these tickets with such carelessness and ease.

We followed a group in front of us down a hallway leading up to the sanctuary. At the entrance to the enormous worship room stood two massive wooden doors with hand-carved images of Jesus on the cross with people crying under him. Jesus's head was tilted back and his eyes wide open looking straight forward; He was still alive. His pupils caught mine, and he seemed to watch me as I passed.

The room was gigantic and warehouse-like. It looked like a basketball court and a half. Long rows of pews formed a half oval around the stage. People occupied every chair. An usher man directed us to the middle of the seventh pew back, a little right of center stage.

I took my seat and looked around at the different people. Everyone was dressed so nicely and all the guys' shirts were tucked. I recognized a few people from school, along with Jackson and his family. They resembled a staircase. Jackson's head, the shortest, situated itself next to his brother's head about two inches above whose head also sat under their mom's, and finally the dad's head completed the stairs.

Several minutes passed as everyone moved about finding their seats. The chattering crowd eventually silenced under the sudden dimming of light.

After a long and suspenseful minute of silence, a man appeared on stage inside a small circle of light that separated him from the rest of the world. The short old man had another shiny hairless head, and he was neatly dressed in a suit. He obviously wasn't part of the play. He blurted out a nervous "he, hello…. HELLO! Welcome to Westhill Baptist Church for an exciting night of drama!" He continued with an introduction for another minute, then said, "And with noooooo… further ado, I am proud to present to the city of St. Joseph… *Heaven's Gates and Hell's Flames!*"

Well that was fairly exciting. I was expecting powerful orchestra music to open up the big showing of *Heaven's Gates and Hell's Flames.* However, the curtain opened up to four teenagers drinking cheap light beer. They looked like they were having a good time. They were laughing and carrying on about this and that. (After a few gulps.) "Ahhhhhh maaaan, we gotta go find us some'n to do." "Mannn I'm havin an awwwwsome time dude. Dude, I love you man."

The acting was horrible. There was a bit more drunken chatter, but that's pretty much what they said. All four of them said something. "We can take my car if you want man?" (Silence and more gulping.) "Heeyyyyyy, but are you sure your alright to drive?" "Yeahhhhhhh man I'm fine really. I've just had like three... seriously."

They acted like they were getting into a car. There was no car there. The driver moved his hands around an invisible wheel as if he were driving. An engine sound kicked in through the loud speakers on either side of the stage. All four of them just tried to act as stupid as possible while they drove, except when they simultaneously jolted hard to their left and started to violently fumble their bodies all about inside the imaginary car. The lights flickered off. At the same time there was screaming, shattering glass, screeching tires, and sounds of shriveling metal.

The whole scene was very dramatic with all the sound effects. And when it was over, all four of the boys lay on the ground dead. After a few seconds of silence while the audience swallowed what just happened, the stage behind the boys revealed itself with bright lights. The first thing was a staircase leading up to what looked like fluffy gold and sparkly white clouds. At the top of the steps stood a woman behind a shimmering white throne. She wore a robe that looked like a cloud, and a halo gently floated above her head on top of a barely visible thin wire. In her hands was a book. She made no sound but paid attention as the boys came into her sight below.

To the right of the lifeless boys on the ground was a fiery red staircase leading down a dark hole under the stage. Around the top of these stairs were black skulls and scary looking flames. The whole area was surrounded by the black and evil looking stuff. Obviously, these were the Gates of Heaven and the Flames of Hell.

I then directed my eyes to the boys who were now starting to move like they had been knocked out and were dizzily reviving. They all looked around at their new surroundings with a terrible look of confusion. They spoke. "What happened man?"

"Man, are we dead?" Their faces suddenly turned to fear. They noticed the woman standing at the top of the steps. She still remained completely silent. "It… it's that place man… It's where you go when you die, and that lady tells us whether we go to Heaven or Hell." "Hey lady," a boy said nervously, "do we get to g-go to Heaven?" "Yeah," another one called, "We've made mistakes in our lives, but… we are good people… really."

The lady's face was still void of emotion. She opened up her big book and carefully flipped through the pages. As she flipped, her face grew gloomy until she stopped and the look on her face was tragic. She looked up with the most innocent and helpless puppy-dog eyes. Tears began to flow as she slowly shook her head from side to side. "What? What's wrong? Aren't we going to Heaven? What have we done? No, wait! NO!"

The woman above buried her face in her hands as thunder clapped and light flickered. All eyes turned to the staircase from Hell as two demonic looking giant men covered in black robes slowly marched up toward the four boys as their knees trembled and their faces went white. With a demon's supernatural strength, they both picked up a boy in each hand. They moved like zombies. The boys wiggled and thrashed but couldn't loosen the Hell zombie's grip as they were carried towards the fiery staircase.

"NOOOOOOOOOOOOOOOOOO!!!" Each boy let out his own last screech of breath as they were dragged down to Hell.

Just as the audience was recovering from the traumatic scene with the boys, the lights quickly dimmed until everything was black for an awkward ten seconds.

The lights came back on the stage, and a happy family sat around a dinner table in the center. They were praying for their meal silently. They were all dressed in nice clothes: the father in slacks with a dress shirt, the pretty mom in a dress, and a little girl about my age in a pink dress. All of them simultaneously ended their prayers and at once began chatting and politely nibbling at their food. "Where is your brother?" The dad spoke the first audible sentence.

"Well, I'm not for sure, I think he said he was going to be late cause he was with a friend," the girl responded.

The mom: "It's getting late. He needs to be coming home."

There was a distant sound of a door slamming, and a teenage boy dressed in all black walked in. He talked sarcastically.

"Hey, you guys already start dinner? You didn't have to wait for me."

The father stood up and said, "Young man where have you been? It's way past dinner time and I haven't gotten a call or anything!"

"Honey, lower your voice," the wife said.

The boy interrupted, "What's wrong with you guys?" "You always have some big problem with whatever I do!"

"Son, we didn't..."

"I hate this family," the boy said. The lights followed him as he stomped out of that room across the stage into what looked like his bedroom. He plunged himself onto his bed and angrily flipped on the TV. Lights moved off of him and went back to the family still at the table. The father's face was buried in his hands as his wife comforted him by rubbing his shoulders. He and the mother looked up when they saw the little girl in front of them praying for her brother.

There was a radio that sat on a counter behind the parents. A hurried voice blared through it, "We have issued a tornado warning for the Tracy County area! Please, everyone stay inside and get to the middle and lowest point of your house immediately and away from all windows. This is a tornado warning for the Tracy County area!"

The mother and father at the table went frantic. The little girl kept praying. Sounds of thunder and lightning roared overhead. The lights went dark. There were sudden flashes of light everywhere coupled with screams and wind noises. The sound of wind dominated! Unidentifiable things blew about on stage. There were screams. Chills broke up through my spine as I watched in awe from my secure seat.

The sounds and the wind died, as well as the screams. The light came back on the stage. The whole family lay on the floor dead, massacred by the storm. They were at the bottom of the steps from before, the gates of Heaven and Hell.

The woman at the top of the steps was emotionless, not reading her book but eerily looking straight ahead. The father came to first, "Honey look!" (waking his family). "It's Heaven! We're in Heaven!" The little girl spoke up, "It's an angel, and she's holding the Book of Life!"

The brother was awake with a dazed and confused frown on his face. The look of disbelief in his face held tight as he darted his eyes around. The angel finally turned down at them and smiled. The brother's mind must have finally caught up with his eyes because he said to his parents with a quiet and fearful voice, "Mom, I... I'm... scared... I'm scared."
The rest of the family acted as if they did not hear. The boy scooted closer to his mom, and she paid no mind. The father blurted out, "Angel! Show us the way to Heaven! Show us the way to Jesus!" The little girl spoke behind him, "Is that the book with the names of followers of Jesus in it? Have our names been written in the Book of Life?" The angel's smile grew as she gave a great nod. She looked at the book as if to reassure herself, and then back up with a smile as big as her face. She held out her arms as she motioned the family to come forward. The whole family got up and walked up the steps toward the angel; the son lagged behind a little, still with a questioning look upon his face.

A passageway in the wall behind the angel revealed itself as gold light filled the theatre. Loud trumpet music kicked in as the mother, father, and then the little girl ascended the staircase and stepped inside the golden passageway. The boy was still a few steps behind when the light and his family rapidly disappeared. "Mom! MOM?" The angel's smile then faded away when she turned toward the boy. "What about me?" he said. "Aren't I in the book along with my family?"

After anxiously flipping through the pages of her book, she frowned deeply like before. She turned once more to the boy as tears began to fall from her eyes. She slowly shook her head back and forth. Once again, the sounds of Hell screeched through the speakers. "But my family is in there!" the boy shouted. "I have to go with them!" "MOM! DAD!!!" He was waving his arms about as tears flew from his helpless eyes. The two demons rose from Hell and marched toward the boy. "NOOOOOO!" he cried. I couldn't move in my seat. "NOOOOOOOOO!"

The demons grabbed at the boy and began to drag him away. *This can't be! The boy has to be with his family!* The family didn't do anything about it though. It was as if they couldn't see him. They were already part of Heaven, and he was already part of Hell. They were good, and he was bad. Away from family, and away from good, for all eternity, he must have been 14.

The rest of the play was similar to the first two scenes: different people would come out, die somehow, and awake next to the angel with the book. She would either light up with bliss or miserably weep as she sent people to Heaven or to Hell. It was incredibly cheesy, but the point was obvious. The people that talked about Jesus… they went to Heaven, and the bad people went to hell. *It makes perfect sense!*

The play ended after the eighth scene. There was no applause, just silence and a few coughs. After about 20 seconds of it, a man walked out on stage. It was the same bald man from before. He looked a little less nervous this time. He started very slowly and paused a lot, "You know… some of those people had no idea. They had not the slightest clue who Jesus was. They did not know what could have been happening in their lives with Him, or even what would happen at the end of their lives without Him. Now they lie in the fiery pits of Hell, forever. No matter how innocent they looked or how special they were to the rest of the

31

world, they are now separated from their friends, their family, and from good, for all eternity. They are in a spot where they can never be seen or noticed by anyone, despite their everlasting cries for help. They will remain in a state of eternal damnation."

"And the people who did make it," he continued. "…they are living in a rich paradise filled with eternal love, joy, and Jesus. The world we live in now is indeed a cruel one. It is filled with sin and brokenness. The Lord came to this cruel world in the form of His son Jesus Christ and gave His own life for all of mankind. He beat death before humankind's very eyes, and He offered us a chance to beat death as well, just as He did. His offer is this, and it still remains."

"For God so loved the world that He gave his only begotten son, and that whosoever believeth in Him shall not perish but have everlasting life." He paused to see the reaction to the scripture, as if it were a new epic phrase no one had ever heard before. "That's John 3:16 ladies and gentlemen. Tonight, I too am giving you all a chance to experience the Lord's offer for yourself. I am giving you a chance to beat death, and live forever with Jesus Christ." *He says it like Christ is this guy's last name…*

"In a few moments, the music is going to play. And what I want you to do is search deep inside yourself for the longing for eternal joy and eternal life. I want you to think about living forever in eternal damnation. Then I want you to think of the Lord's offer again, and how He can save you from death if you are just willing to follow Him. In a moment the music will play, and that is your chance to come forward and accept that offer. There are deacons standing up here at the front. Come to one of them and they will talk to you about the important decision you are about to make. Leave behind your previous life. Do it, and you will be saved forever. Live without accepting God's gift and you will surely go to HELL: away from friends, family, and good for all eternity!"

The music started.

Goodness! What was I to do? How was I to proceed? Hell looked like the worst place ever. All along I thought I was Heaven-bound; that not struggling against my parents when they made me go to church every week was enough for Heaven. *If I went to hell, no one could hear me. I would be there forever. If I don't walk up now and accept the Lord like the bald man said, then I will go to Hell! If I do, then I will go to Heaven! Well I surely don't want to go to Hell.*

I looked around, for I feared that my friends would think I was weird if I went up. Others started to get up and walk forward though. *OK...This is it. You can do this!* I felt myself getting up. I put one leg in front of the other, and soon I knew for sure that I was on my way to Heaven. I walked up to the front of the stage while the music played. I noticed a number of people silently walking to stand by me. Once everyone had made their way up, the music faded out. The bald man looked at us, smiled, and said, "Will you pray with me."

After saying "Amen," he told us to follow an usher to a separate room behind the stage. I looked back at my parents in the seats, who were smiling proudly as if I'd just given a breakthrough performance at an elementary school play. They nodded for me to go ahead.

A man walked up to me and cheerfully urged me to follow. I looked up at his face as I followed him. This man wasn't bald. He had a nice head of shiny brown hair. He was as tall as Dad, around 6 feet, and his skin wrapped so tightly around his face that it stretched his giant smile. He also had a deep crevice in the middle of his chin. I would have mistaken it for a butt if the rest of his face were not there. He had giant hearing aids behind his shiny ears that made them stick out. However, this guy didn't look old enough for hearing aids. *Only old people wear hearing aids...* I enjoyed the thought that I would never have to deal with such nonsense. I'd say this guy was in his mid-30's. *That is not old enough for hearing aids...*

After examining the extreme smile and extreme features of his face, I determined that this man was very happy. I followed him to a back room. We stopped and he knelt down on his right knee to my level. There were plenty of other people being talked at by various ushers. I think I had the only one with hair. "Now what's your name, son?" the kneeling man asked me. I proudly replied, "My name is John Christian Cathcart..." feeling extra pleased to present to him that my middle name was indeed Christian, like I was the perfect kid for the part.

"Well John, I want you to know that you're taking the most important step in your life that you will ever take. You are a child of Jesus now, and you will experience His love throughout your new life." *New life... This is great!* "John, I'm so glad you're going to know Jesus. You know, Jesus is too... You understand that, right? Jesus is so in love with you John. Jesus; you will be with Him now forever."

Jesus... oh! I get it now! The guy sounded like a prissy high-school girl saying "like" in every sentence. He repeated "Jesus" as if it were some scheme of his to subliminally implant the word in my head. "Do you mind if I pray with you?" he asked.

"No," I said politely. He clasped hands together. He created a heart shape where his hands met, folded together in the crescent at the top. He suspended them about two inches out from his chest, his fingers centered below the deep gorge in his chin. He slowly bent his forehead down to them. Red flushed through his cheeks as his smile widened, like he had just successfully completed the absolute perfect position for prayer. After observing his carefully placed move, I mimicked. A few seconds of silence passed, with the exception of the loud chatter from others in the room being branded "Jesus!"

The man spoke up slowly and dramatically, "Oh... Heavenly Father, lay your blessings on this young man next to me. He has chosen to follow you, Lord. He has decided to leave all of his worries, all of his woes, and all of his regrets behind, get up off of his poor feet, and follow you Lord. Lord, bless young John's journey through the river of life, and may great things come to him. We pray that you will graciously accept John's request to follow you forever... Amen."

I repeated, "Amen." I looked up at the man who smiled really big directly into my eyes. I looked down and thought about what had just happened. *OK, I am a Christian now! I am going to go to Heaven!* It seemed to me, at that moment, considering the intensity of the man's prayer, and the presumed value of the life-changing moment, that I should have felt a little more excited than I did. I concentrated hard on my feelings inside and out. I expected to feel some enlightening, some divine change at least in my body temperature or something, but I just noticed the itches on my arms and legs.

I looked back up at the man who was now standing with a big smile on his face. He whipped out his hand so quickly it made me blink. In it were some booklets. "Here, these verses and devotionals will help you get started on your journey with Jesus." I looked at one of the little paper booklets he handed me, "Getting Started in Your Faith."

Although he was not a huge man, he looked so experienced and superior to me and my little "getting started" booklets. His hearing aids looked small all of the sudden. "John," his bright smile dimmed to seriousness, "I want you to remember this always. The hand of God is always there, no matter where you may be. The hand of God will always be right there for you; you simply have to reach for it. In your darkest, lowest moments John, reach for the hand of God." He patted me on the back, said "Good luck in your journey John," and walked away anxiously looking for someone else to brand.

I was set. I was on my own now. I gathered my stack of booklets, turned, and looked ahead to the door back out to the stage - to the new world. I then began my new journey into Christianity, my journey with Jesus. *My life is going to be great, easy, and I will always be happy, they said.* As I passed through the door, I think the feeling caught up with me, the excitement, the Christianity. It was like crossing a legendary veil into an entirely different dimension. *It's the climax of my life! I think I'm feeling it! Man... I am totally feeling it. I can't believe it... my life now - it is going to be great!*

3
Reward

September 1997

They put me to sleep Saturday morning at six. Around noon, my eyes opened to a new, unfocused and untouched *world.*

Dr. Mujica did an admirable job on my head. Inside of a half-foot incision behind my right ear, he found the tumor on my cerebellum and cut most of it away with a special knife. Some doctors refer to the process as "debulking" the tumor.

My dad explained to me, "Well, a brain kind of looks like a big glob of jelly - gray jelly. The tumor looks like a glob of red jelly stuck to it. Imagine if you made a peanut butter and jelly sandwich, and while applying the grape jelly, you realize that you spilled a blob of strawberry jelly in the midst of grape jelly. In your efforts to remove the strawberry jelly as much as possible without scooping up any grape jelly, you would essentially be debulking a brain tumor."

Dr. Mujica cut out the red jelly, scooped it into a baggie, and sent it off to a laboratory to be examined. The red jelly was big enough and hard enough that it was squishing my brain against my skull as both jellies tried to fit, but there wasn't enough room... too much peanut butter... I would have surely died after another couple days or so of tumor growth if it were not for Dr. Mujica. The tumor would have basically squashed my brain.

Most people who have this big of a tumor taken off of the base of their brain have problems. The spot where the tumor departs becomes a gorge of empty space, and the brain usually slumps down into it. When that happens, the brain distorts and the patient has motor troubles such as clumsiness, slurred speech, and poor hand-eye coordination. Those people are temporarily mentally disabled. My tumor was huge and at the bottom of my head. It claimed a giant space that was once my brain's. It was

36

almost a sure thing that my brain would slump to fill the spot. Miraculously, my brain stayed upright after surgery.

The cerebellum is the region of the brain where the tumor was debulked, distinctly separate from the main two lobes. This is the part of the brain that controls balance and coordination. Though my whole brain didn't slump down, my cerebellum was still scraped up. Therefore, after a day or two, when I was physically able to get up, I couldn't walk straight at all. All of my movements were slow, weak, and unbalanced. If I had been strong enough to stand without people holding me up, then I would have fallen forward, backward, or to a side without realizing it. My speech slurred as well. I sounded as if my mouth was full of cotton.

They moved me to an intensive care unit hours after I woke from surgery. The intensive care room was similar to the other rooms, only nurses paid more attention to it for patients recovering from intense hits on their body, such as brain surgery. It also housed a few more interesting tools. The ICU was sealed off from the infectious hallway with an automatic, double glass doorway. There was a small TV in the corner, and next to my bed were two cheap recliners for my parents to sleep in. They were blue.

I wore a paper-mâché-like helmet bundled around my head and partly over my face. Everything was incredibly swollen. My purple cheeks puffed out like cotton candy. My throat had swelled so badly that I had trouble breathing. There was a ringing in my ears. It was too high-pitched to compare to anything, and loud enough to be annoying.

Things still hurt from the catheter. I couldn't pee on my own because my bladder was numb, and I couldn't stand on my own so I had to have someone hold me upright whenever I tried to pee. Though in a strange, numbed, drugged state, I felt hot blood throbbing through all of my limbs. My body was an army all connected to one general - my brain. The general had been nearly shot to death so the entire rest of the army went mad. I think that many cells all throughout my body were confused and didn't know what to do, so they just kept banging their heads against the walls of my insides.

Each day was long as I recovered cell by cell in the giant hospital in St. Joseph, and I don't remember how I got through them. I would lie for hours and hours dumbly gazing at the ceiling. The television hurt my eyes most of the time and listening to it gave me a headache. So I'd lay in silence. In absence of other sound, the ringing in my ears would get so strong it would trance me to sleep.

My family was in the ICU room as much as they could be. Mom was in there 24/7. I would speak when I was awake and able to. Mom and I talked about school and friends. When the rest of my family was there, I would entertain them with jokes I came up with when I was high off the drugs. I remember Morphine, which was incredible. When on morphine, I would often float off of the bed and drift around the room. Sometimes, I'd look down and see my body on the bed, sleeping and smiling. Aside the chaos in my world, morphine took me to a zen-like calm. It's not quite the feeling of being really drunk, but it's close, but I'd say intensely relaxed… very intensely. It made my veins feel like they were vibrating, and it sent a mysterious buzz through my drowsy face.

• • •

Now how in the world did this just happen? I'm Christian now… I felt it when I walked out of that door. This is not supposed to happen to me. Meditating on my morphine, I would see Him, God, up in the sky looking at me. He kept a straight face, not saying a word. I silently stared back. All the features of His face were fuzzy, but I could tell it was incredibly detailed, and I knew it was Him. He knew where I was, and He knew that I had recently given Him my life. *Some reward for accepting Jesus… Some rewarding and satisfying life. This sucks.* I didn't understand; I went to church, I believed in God, what else? I thought hard about this, about how bad my new life was, and how much better off everyone else's was. *It's not like I've been off raping and killing. The killers aren't lying in a hospital bed. Pedafiles surely aren't having tubes jammed up their bladders.*

After a few days of this half-consciousness, they moved me out of ICU into a regular hospital room on the floor, where stampedes of friends lined up outside of my room every day to show their love and respect for me and my family.

Being exhausted and in pain the whole time, it was hard to entertain every crowd. It was embarrassing for everyone to see me the way I was. I still had my papier-mâché helmet on. I was dressed in a corny butt exposing hospital gown, and my face was swollen purple like Violet, the little blueberry girl from *Willy Wonka and the Chocolate Factory.*

The nurse would come in every once in a while and dilute the crowd by shooing people away. My family was in no better condition to entertain guests than I was. Many times there would be a party of people in my room, and I would have to go to the bathroom. Imagine telling everyone to leave because your dad has to help you get up and go. My dad and I tried to make up little excuses for people to leave, hiding the fact that I had to pee. We would say things like, "John's getting pretty tired," "Oh it is time for the doctor to come in," better yet, "Oh it's time to poop everyone, and John can't do it by himself, so can you all just pitch in an extra hand?"

On the last day, Dr. Mujica came in and took away my helmet that was crusted with old blood, sweat, and a gross puss-like fluid. It sure felt good to get air to my sticky swollen head. I reached up to feel around. It was a fresh battlefield: a barren dry ground with bumps and craters left from the chaos, and lonely patches of scraggily hair that survived. To my surprise, however, there was still a lot of hair in the front of my head. I was under the impression that my head would be bald. Although it looked ridiculous, and had to eventually come off, I was happy that some was still there.

As my fingers ventured over the surface of my newly landscaped head, they ran into some large Band-Aids at each corner of the top of my head. The bandages covered four large bumps that were very tender, like they'd been dug into as well.

"That's where we screwed in metal rods. They held your head perfectly still and in place during the surgery." Mujica said. *Fantastic...*

My fingers moved on. The entire back of my head was numb. I lightly and bravely ran a finger over the long incision. I felt staples. They weren't office staples, but big heavy-duty staples you would put into a thick piece of wood. The staples held the two separated flaps of skin tightly together so that skin around my cut was stretched like a balloon.

"There are twenty of them." Dr. Mujica said as he watched me explore my new head. "Are you all right with it?" *Of course I'm not alright with it.* My dad spoke up for me, "You did a great job, thank you." To my hand, it felt like everything was plastic. It wasn't tingly with a needle feeling, like when your foot is asleep. It really felt like the back of my head was not supposed to be there; I could feel it with my hand, but my head couldn't feel my hand rubbing on it.

"Wonderful!" Mujica said. "Are you guys all ready to go home?" *Those are words I've been waiting for!* I'd already missed enough of my first month at middle school. My parents instantly started packing to go home and to get back on with our lives that were going so smoothly before, but somehow got rudely bumped by a big fat blob of jelly in my head. They rolled me out in a wheelchair.

Despite how anxious I was to get on with my life, I wasn't going to be ready to go to school for about two weeks. But I was happy to be getting home where I could recover in peace. However, I didn't feel like it was all over just like that. It was just... things this big don't usually vanish without a trace. I tried not to worry too much about it.

"Are you guys all ready to go home?" The words resounded in my head. Finally… with a chunk of my brain gone and out of the picture I was ready to move on.

●●●

People visited frequently during the afternoon. When my friends got out of school around 3:00, the most visitors would come by.

Jackson and three other friends from school came into my room one day. They all had completely shaved their heads. They did it so that I wouldn't feel weird when I came back to school with a bald head. In surgery, only part of my head had been shaved. My friends didn't think it was that funny when they walked in my room and found that I still had half a head of good hair.

People would bring a whole bunch of gifts, mostly candy and balloons. I was in no condition to eat candy, but happy to get it. Mom, Kristin, and Casey really liked it, so they would eat it all.

●●●

Every day went by the same way. With every passing moment, my balance and my head grew slightly more tolerable. The little TV room adjacent to the long wooden hallway in my house was perfect for me. I would relax on the little red couch and watch action movies all day. I love to watch Jackie Chan. I have a whole collection of timeless Jackie Chan films. His cheesy comedy is great, along with his amazing moves and use of everyday objects as weapons. It's like, whatever gets in his way, he always turns it around and finds a way to use it to his advantage. I dreamed of being his sidekick one day.

When I wasn't watching movies or entertaining guests, I would try to do my homework. I was missing school, but the teachers didn't forget about me. Every day at about 4:00, Jackson would show up at my door with a handful of schoolwork. He would stay for at least an hour. We would sit at my dining room table and he would tell me about school that day. "So what happened at school today?" Most of the time he responded "Not much." He would help me understand the schoolwork. He was always patient with me, because he was scared he would go too fast and violate the boundaries of my weariness. The work was hard for me because my head got tired quickly. I would easily get dizzy, and Jackson wouldn't understand how to react, but he would stay.

Nearly ten days had passed at home while I slowly regained half of my alertness and coordination. The swelling of my face and my throat had gone down enough by then that I could eat simple things.

One afternoon I was having a bowl of cereal in the TV room when Mom popped in, "It's almost time to go check up with Dr. Mujica. Are you ready?" *All right! He's going to take my staples out and tell me I can go back to school.*

I was a little scared about getting the staples pulled out of my head, but I was all for anything that would get me a step back to being normal. Normal people just don't wear staples.

· · ·

After an hour or so past my scheduled appointment time, I woke up on a blue chair in the waiting room to hear my name called to go to Dr. Mujica's office. The lady with the afro from before escorted me into the small square room. It seemed I waited another half hour for Mujica to come in.

The door finally swung open, but Mujica didn't pop through it. A few seconds passed before he did come in, as though he had purposely stalled. The door and Dr. Mujica weren't on the same time frame. "How are you doing John?" he asked. "How does your head feel?" He held a tool in his hand that looked like a bottle cap opener. "Looks like those things are wanting to come

42

out of there." I was excited to have my head to myself again without any foreign objects in it.

He came over to me and reached for the back of my head. I could feel him press hard with each prick of a staple. I couldn't really feel the staples coming out, but I could feel that something was happening. It was a strange feeling, but it didn't take long. "All done!" he said before it seemed like he could have been. "Now the only things left in there are three metal screws we used to bind your skull back together in surgery. After a month or two they should dissolve in your head. *Great, now I could enjoy radio within the comfort of my own head.*

"OK," I said. "Now, can I have Mom and Dad step outside with me for a minute?" he asked. They looked at me, then looked back at each other and nodded. My parents walked out with Mujica, leaving me to dwell alone in the sterile confines of the exam room and the disbelief that we were going to walk out of here with our lives the happy same as before.

· · ·

It was malignant… the name they granted my wicked tumor. A brain tumor is an evil mass of abnormal cells that have grown out of control. There are benign (non-cancerous) tumors, and malignant tumors. Malignancy is cancer. There are several types of malignant tumors that grow in children's brains. Astrocytoma tumors are the most common, and at the same time most deadly. These tumors usually grow within the brain and intermingle with normal brain tissue. Probably the second most common malignant tumor to occur within children is called Primitive Neuroectodermal (PNET). When these tumors arise in the cerebellum, they are called Medulloblastomas.

Medulloblastoma is the tumor that I had. It appeared in the posterior fossa region of my brain (the lower back, or cerebellum). This tumor usually appears in children within the first decade of their lifetime; most occur when children are five or six. I was 12.

43

The exact cell that goes haywire and becomes this tumor is unknown. These types of tumors are very eager to spread to other areas of the brain and to take an unauthorized journey down the spinal chord.

The first step in treatment for these tumors is the debulking. Most of these cancerous tumors can be completely removed. After surgery, tests are done to see if there is any residual cancer left at the operating site and if and where it has spread. The doctors saw little evidence of my cancer after the surgery and determined my tumor to have been 90% dubulked. This being great news, I continued with the normal treatment. The second step in treatment is low-dose radiation. Medulloblastomas are extremely sensitive to radiation. After the radiation, patients usually receive four rounds of low-dose chemotherapy to destroy any remains of cancer that might have fallen throughout the body.

The way chemotherapy works is quite brutal. It seeks out any cell in the body that is attempting to divide or grow and destroys them. Chemo kills any cells that are rapidly dividing, such as cancer cells, but it also kills blood cells or any innocent healthy cells in active growth. Thus, chemotherapy produces drastic side effects.

• • •

I have cancer… cancer… me. The words sounded so unreal, like words that both existed, but in two completely different contexts and dimensions. Beef and breakfast cereal are two completely different words that no one would ever find together in a reasonable sentence. "Cancer" and "me:" the two words are parts of different worlds that could never cross.

However, I somewhat expected it. I mean… brain surgery isn't just an everyday problem that people deal with once, and then it goes away like a scrape on your knee. Something else was behind it like an infomercial: "But wait! There's more!"

So they pinned me with cancer, and I had to be treated - sent away like a rabid dog, or a drug-addict - to be repaired like a misfit Christmas toy. "John," Dad looked me sternly in the eye and said, "The doctors tell me that you need to go to a hospital far away to be treated. The place is called St. Jude's Children's Research Hospital. It's in Memphis, Tennessee. The people there specialize in treating what you have. You'll be there for nearly a year."

Memphis, Tennessee... Memphis, Tennessee... The name resounded through my sore head over and over. *Memphis, Tennessee...* I couldn't even think of where this place was on the map, let alone think about leaving everything to go live there for a year while I get treated for cancer. *A fricking year! No! I have school! I have friends! I can't just drop out. I have a life! No! No! No! What's happening to me? I don't even say cuss words! I'm a Christian... I'm going to Heaven for God sake!*

After Dad told me where I had to go, I didn't say anything except "yeah" and "OK". Then I walked away to my little TV room with the red leather love seat to sit by myself. Dad didn't follow me. I didn't want him to. He knew I had to take time to think. Everything that was happening - it was an incredible amount to swallow all too fast, especially considering my throat was still halfway swollen from the debulking.

I curled up on the red love seat. I recognized the texture of the loud creaks approaching from the old wooden hallway. The door opened a crack and Mr. Mischief waddled in. He hopped up to fill the other half of the love seat. He instantly curled up to me and started purring, as if identifying my state of uneasiness and wanting to comfort me. I just stared at the ceiling with my arm around Mr. Mischief.

I struggled to wake up to any type of reality. I knew it was a nightmare. I've had dreams like this before where something tragic happens, like a loved one dies, or you do something horrible. But I have always woken up from them, usually with tears in my eyes, but I wake up and it's gone. If I woke up, it would all be gone. I hit myself hard, pinched my nipple, banged my head, and eventually drifted to sleep in a pillow of my own tears.

I felt somehow like it was my fault. I can still remember the voices I heard that night. They weren't loud voices other people could hear, but more like something for me only. "Congratulations for becoming a Christian… Sucker!"

…

My grandparents owned a fancy hotel in Branson, Missouri. To try and make our trip to Memphis as smooth and luxurious as possible, my grandpa drove my parents and I down to Memphis in his stretch limo. There was a black leather L-shaped couch curling around the inside. There was a small black TV with a built-in VCR, a shiny black mini fridge, a wine cooler, a wine storage bin, and several cup holders. The black ceiling was covered in gold lights that we controlled with a dimmer switch. In the back there was another couch facing the front. My grandmother drove behind us in Dad's Lincoln so that they could drop us off in Memphis and drive back to Branson with the limo. That way, Dad could make it back to work in a few days.

When we first arrived in Memphis, we went straight to my new home, St. Jude Children's Research Hospital. St. Jude is not just any hospital; there is a good reason I was told to come here, even though there are great children's hospitals in my area. Kids from all over the world come here to be treated for cancers. St. Jude is the big time. It's on commercials, frequently visited by celebrities, and the hospital is supported by millions of people around the globe.

There were alternative living options offered by St. Jude Hospital such as the Ronald McDonald House or the Target House, all paid for by donations. The Ronald McDonald House is a home where patients doomed for a long-term stay can live for free during their treatments. The large apartment-filled house is less than a few blocks from the hospital, so patients can easily be shuttled back and forth throughout the day. The Target House is the same, but farther away from the hospital. Though these options were nice, we wanted our life to be as less hospital-like as possible. So we found an apartment in Germantown, a Memphis suburb about 30 minutes away. Every day for the first several weeks, we drove to the hospital for numerous tests and scans, and the insertion of the dreadful line.

The line was a thick IV they stuck in my chest. It went into a large vein, referred to by the doctors as the superior vena cava, right by my heart. After two weeks of tests and the line, we came every day for six weeks of radiation therapy, which was supposed to burn away any remaining red jelly in my brain or any cancer cells venturing down my spine. The radiation caused constant nausea, an extreme lack of energy, and an extreme lack of self. Radiation made me an intense sort of sick that can't be experienced anywhere else. It's not only an awkward and terrible physical feeling like your guts are frying, but emotional, like your thoughts are frying too.

After six weeks of radiation, I took a long break to recover during Christmas. I enjoyed going home and seeing my close friends. In January, I went back to Memphis and started chemotherapy; four rounds with stem cell support/transplant each month. This was worse than the radiation. Chemo consisted of hardcore drugs that flushed my body and killed every dividing cell, causing a world of problems and six months of a sort of unbearable nauseating torture.

Stem cells are essential to a recovery, and stem cells are found in bone marrow. My specific chemotherapy dissolves and rots bone marrow, so before a round of chemo, I would have a good amount of bone marrow sucked out and stored in freezers. After each round of chemo, my bone marrow was given back to me so that the stem cells would help me recover - thus completing a bone marrow transplant.

Despite my miserable physical life, I still had middle school to deal with. There was no way I was going to completely drop my life and let myself fall behind simply because of a little cancer trouble. I stayed in school. Every week Nancy Siemens, the nurse at Bode Middle School, would send me a packet full of lessons and homework to do. The packets held all the stuff the other kids did back home. I was to do them all like normal. The only thing was,

47

I didn't have a teacher. I had to rely on the books entirely. Reading made my head throb, but the pages were surprisingly vomit resistant.

I even took all the tests. Mom acted as my teacher; she'd make sure I never cheated and helped me out when I had trouble.

Mom left her friends and her responsibilities to come take care of me in Memphis. Kristin dropped out of Kansas University in the middle of the semester and came to live with us. Cancer had ripped us from Casey, who was in her last year of high school at home, and from Dad, who stayed home to work.

4

Radiation 101

November 1997

These blue chairs were stained with years of radiation patients. The radiation/MRI waiting room welcomed Mom, Kristin and I daily. They were really couches, the blue chairs, because they all connected with red poles. I called them couch-chairs. Beneath them, scratchy white tiles covered the open floor.

Red and white was the typical color scheme of St. Jude Children's Hospital in 1997 - not really straight white, maybe an extremely light beige - but white is the first color that comes to mind. I think it was hardly an appropriate choice of colors for a children's hospital. The colors were so hard and forceful, annoyingly stable and sharp. With the nauseating feeling one gets from chemotherapy or radiation treatments, white and red only seemed to add to the discomfort.

However, in the waiting rooms, the chairs were a faded light blue. The room was off the side of a large hallway where doctors and nurses frequently traveled, so the air was open and echoic. Children sat with one or two of their parents all around on the couch-chairs, usually as close as possible to them. Some had a gloomy frown and tired eyes. All were bald and frightened for their lives.

I curled up to Mom with my small bald head resting on her shoulder while she read, and my sister and I stared at the door to the radiation therapy department. It was extremely bright in there. We were waiting for a nurse to pop her head out of it and call the next name to come enter the light and have their daily source of concentrated radiation rays burn through traces of cancer in their bodies. I usually tried to keep a happy face. I felt like I was supposed to be mature since I was 12, and most of the other kids around were much younger. I felt like I should have been more able to handle the pulsing nausea that we all felt in that waiting room. I felt like I should set a good example and be happy.

Every once in a while I'd be looking around and I'd start to think about some of the faint stains on the couches, about their owners, about their stories. After nearly an hour of waiting impatiently, the sound of my name woke me from my daze. Mom looked at me, "Oh, Honey, they're calling you back. We'll see you in a little bit." The whole time waiting, I built up a large amount of anticipation to go through the whole process again. I just couldn't wait to digest the poison rays. I got up and followed the lady through the door into the pupil-piercing void of light beyond.

• • •

I was used to it by now. It had been three weeks of radiation treatment every day, Monday through Friday, roughly at 9:00 in the morning.

It took nearly an hour to get to the hospital when we would go through town from our apartment in Germantown. We normally worked our way through the traffic jams of morning rush hour. Sometimes it was just Mom and I. Kristin was taking classes at the University of Tennessee in Memphis, and she found a job teaching ballroom dance.

The apartment was a big change for us. Back in St. Joe, we had one of the oldest and classiest mansions in town. The two bedrooms, single bath, and a connected living / dining room was hardly comparable to our house in St. Joe. However, it was our house for the duration of my treatment that year. Kristin, who came from the closet-like dorms at Kansas University, probably enjoyed the space we had.

I made my morning routine as close to that of home as possible. I got up every morning with a bowl of cereal and a good cartoon, usually *Sonic the Hedgehog*. The daily trip to school was replaced with a long drive to the hospital to spend the day getting radiated and doing various other appointments and tests. A lot of times we would take scenic roads into town instead of the highway.

...

"We need to clean your line before we go sweetie." *Oh God, nooo...* "We don't need to change it!" I shouted in disbelief. "Please no..." I looked at Mom and my bottom lip grew. My hand unconsciously went to cover the line on my chest, protecting it from her.

The line was a snake coming out of my heart. It was the giant IV that they stuck through my chest and into one of the big veins that went straight to my heart. It really looked like a small snake, and it stayed in at all times during my treatment. They would take blood from it and shoot medicine through it. It was just like a regular IV in any arm, but it was heavy-duty and long-term. Since it had to stay in for months, it had to be cleaned every other day. This involved carefully removing the bandages around it, wiping it clean with alcohol and betadine, flushing it with heparin (pepper-like liquid) to keep it open and working, then carefully placing a new clean bandage over it. The line was very unstable. It was stuck deep within my chest, not held in by nails or scotch tape or anything. It was only slightly stabilized by the tissues within my skin that clung to it, imagining it was some foreign savior sent inside to set things right. The line can essentially move in and out freely if tugged, which is extremely painful and sort of sick. Though it was held in place by tight bandages, I kept my hand over it at all times.

The bandages around it go bad quickly, so we had to put new ones on frequently. When Mom changed it, she took off every bandage, actually lifting up the line like a limp arm and poking little cotton swabs of alcohol around and underneath it to clean my skin. It was extremely uncomfortable. While she worked, my eyes stared as intently on the tube's entrance to my chest as a dog would at your dinner. I would let out a bellow if I saw the slimy snake move in or out at all. I hated my line and I wanted to burn it away from my chest every time I saw it. Picture having to carry a knife in your back everywhere you go, but you had to leave it in and sterilize the wound everyday.

After the changing of my bandages and cleaning of my line, we started the long trip to the great shrine St. Jude Children's Research Hospital in downtown Memphis.

We drove down Poplar Avenue, which spans the 30 miles between Memphis and Germantown. We were nearly halfway there when we passed Sun Studios, the little yellow recording studio where Elvis Presley played "That's All Right." We passed this everyday, and I could see him in there. Elvis was leaning on a bench, strumming his guitar in the studio. He looked up at me through the window and winked. He probably knew what was going on. He knew I was on my way to the hospital. I winked back. I think Elvis and I held some unspoken connection in Memphis. Memphis is a very spirit heavy city. You'll see if you go there.

We were approaching our destination and from far away, the great towers of the hospital loomed above. It was a giant castle. We pulled up to the daunting gates at the entrance. A guard walked out of the little hut next to the drive. He glanced at the patient parking tag hanging from our windshield, and waved to let us pass through into the grounds of the hospital.

Radiation messed with my senses. A lot of food didn't taste the same at that time, and my sense of smell was like that of a dog. I smelled the most discrete farts. I sensed body odors from five feet away. I learned to hold my breath every time we entered the hospital, because the field of air within the parking garage under the hospital and around the front door carried unusual nauseating stenches. It smelled similar to the creamy dust scent present when someone is nailing into concrete, or when firing up a kiln. If I didn't hold my breath when I walked through the entrance, I hurled.

Upon entering, we came to a pair of sweet plump ladies at the registration desks. Every patient checked in with them each day in order to get their hospital schedules and wristbands. I became a regular, and the happy ladies started to learn my name. One lady started to chant, grin wildly, and pump her shoulders when she saw me walk in, "Hey everybody! I said John is in the House! John is in the House!!"

The first thing on our schedule was called assessment/triage. A/T was first visit of the day for every patient. It's where they checked your vital signs. Our next appointment was with the D-clinic. The D-clinic was the specific clinic in the hospital that dealt with my type of cancer. They also had A, B, C, and E. The happy lady at the desk slapped on a bright blue wristband. Blue was the color for Monday, and each following day of the week was coded with a different color wristband.

We then went to A/T. Mom and I walked through a hall to the right of the ladies and entered the giant outpatient waiting room, the busiest waiting room in the hospital. It was the waiting room for all the major clinics A-D, the Pulmonary Function testing, the Audiology Clinic, and the Eye Center. The room was shaped like a large triangle. It was constantly crowded with small children and their parents waiting for various appointments. These people were from many different parts of the world. They were all yapping gibberish in their own languages, and their kids were either running around playing with the toys St. Jude provided, playing games with their hands, trying to sleep gloomily on their mother's shoulder, or crying loudly under their own woe and misery. The parents usually tried to sleep or read, though a very difficult task in the midst of such a nerve-racking atmosphere.

This was the typical scene of the main waiting room at St. Jude's during the day. Everyone seems to just go crazy while waiting until their name is called over the loudspeaker to come back into their specific clinic. After just a few days, I had grown easily annoyed by everything in there. *The kids are everywhere. There's too many of them...* I would repeat to myself as the weight of my own butt grew heavier with every lengthy minute on the light blue couch/chairs with dark stains.

• • •

The wind was so loud, thundering clouds and lightning jolted with each pounding step. The elephant had flesh like a human. He was carrying me somewhere. I knew he wasn't a human, but he must have been disguising himself as one for some reason. I guess that way I felt more comfortable riding him. The wind hit my face violently, like a tornado. Nothing hurt. The wind hit my elephant with the same force. I thought I saw his eyes wincing though, as his face struggled against the debris. I felt sorry for him. We were going so fast. We were in some sort of city. There were buildings and cars all around us, but they seemed so far away, untouchable but very real - so untouchable that the world below had a different texture, similar to a deep-grade oil painting. We were above it. I was surfing on my elephant now. I turned around and realized there was someone behind me on the elephant as well. It was a soldier in camouflage like he was at war. He smiled at me and stared for quite some time without saying a word. I opened my eyes and the wind suddenly got sucked into silence.

• • •

It was Mom. The sound of the hospital uncomfortably rushed into my ears like a light flipped on after hours of darkness. She was waking me up because I had been called back. I was a little upset I was taken from my dream world.

I wiped my eyes and experienced a light-headed whoosh as I staggered to a stand. Mom and I escaped the noisy waiting room and walked behind an unmarked door next to the A-clinic quarters to a long hallway with a series of small rooms. The walls, and floors were covered with creamy white squares. The ceiling was white; the atmosphere screamed sterility. Toward the end of the small hallway were two doors across from each other. Above one closed entrance, a sign read *Pulmonary Function*. The sign above the room next to it read *Echo/EKG*. From inside the Echo/EKG room, an attractive African-American lady flashed her bright white teeth at us.

"Hi John! How yah doin' Mom?" All of the staff referred to parents of patients as "Mom" or "Dad." I think this provided for a more personal relationship between staff and kids, something I believe should be mandatory at a children's hospital.

"Oh wonderful, thank you!" Mom replied in that halfway fake happy tone that moms sometimes use when talking small talk with other moms.

"We're more than halfway through the radiation treatments!" she said to the Echo/EKG lady.

"Well that's great news!" The lady turned her attention to me without looking. "...and what about you John? I bet you're getting excited. How are you doing?" Her eyes remained down at her desk while organizing some papers and looking through the files in my chart. I was already sitting on the tissue-covered bed in the middle of the room.

"Of course, I'm doing wonderful!" It seemed an automated reply. She got up from her desk and walked towards the side of my bed while still examining my chart. Everywhere I went in the hospital, my chart was sent as well. My chart was a giant book of personal medical records and history. I guess if I had a book of life like the angel at Heaven's Gates, then that would be it.

"Aaaaaaall... right John, let's go ahead and get you started so we can get you out of here to enjoy this beautiful day. Is this your last appointment?" The lady asked. She stretched out her "alls". Mom answered for me, "Oh no. Looks like they have us up for two more today, but hopefully we'll be out in time to enjoy the sun."

"Aaaaaaall right John, if you'll just slip your shirt off, we'll get you hooked up." *Such a cheerful attitude for such a statement.* The first part of this appointment was the EKG. During EKG, the lady stuck several round stickers to certain parts of my chest, shoulders, and arms. The stickers were attached to cables that went back to the computers. They were actually electrodes that measured electronic forces from my heart as it pumped blood throughout my body. It was like the electrodes on E.T. when they wired him up in the hospital.

I was fine with the EKG. It didn't hurt at all; it slightly tickled more than anything. However I didn't look forward to the next part, the Echo (Echocardiogram). This procedure was also for my heart.

"Ok John let's get these stickers off of you and we'll pull out the *wand.*" The word sounded so daunting. We called it the wand because it could magically see inside of me when she rubbed it over my chest the right way. The wand is a short rod also connected to the computers by a series of cables. It has a ball-shaped light at the end of it. It's the same thing used for ultrasounds. She fiddled around with the wand for a minute, untangling chords and typing things in the computer.

Before she started, she reached her hand down into a little jar and scooped up a blob of bluish goo, plopped it on my chest right in front of my eyes, similar to a high school lunch lady who forcefully plops a blob of cheesy mashed potatoes on your plate. The goo helps maintain good contact with the skin. Then she pushed the wand down in the splotch of goo. My eyes winced as she pressed down hard on my chest with the wand. I could feel it right over my line; it was a sickening and painful experience. It felt like she was pushing the line deeper into my chest by putting all of her weight on top of it.

The wand shot a special type of light into my skin that bounced off of my arteries and other insides. The light reflected back through to the wand and finally to the computer. The computer then made an electronic image of the light information (my heart).

The room was dark like a theatre. As the lady forcefully moved the wand around my chest, the main arteries near my heart were displayed on a small monitor next to my bed. The black and white arteries looked like microscopic pictures of the inside of a worm in science textbooks. It was kind of a gross feeling to see what was going on inside of me at the present moment; my own innards at work. I concentrated most of the time on flexing my chest so that it would hold up my line and lessen the pain as much as possible.

56

For just about a minute, however, she would move the wand directly over my heart, to an area of me where the line couldn't go. During that time, I could relax my muscles and pay more attention to the screen over my shoulder.

I was looking at a black and white image of my heart; pumping in and out. *Ugly old thing really... Doesn't look like a heart at all...* I could see it go in and out, and with each pump, I felt the beat from my chest up against the pressure of the wand. The feeling and the image were in sync. I remember a couple of times I would think to myself, after staring at my heart for a few seconds: *despite the Hell that this is, that this whole thing is... how many people in the world get a chance to stare into the panting eyes of their own heart and feel it at the same time?*

· · ·

As soon as we got home, I ran to the bathroom to hurl. The radiation gave me a nausea that stayed in me all of the time. It randomly triggered my irritated innards to erupt at least two or three times a day. It became a routine after a while, and it was part of my daily activities.

Mom opened up the door and I burst through, running towards the bathroom. "Oh honey..." Mom said. She knew it wouldn't leave me alone. The burn from the rays had also turned all of my favorite foods to a gray mush. Everything tasted wrong. I never felt hungry. I couldn't stand having food in my mouth; food just made me hurl.

The bland bathroom walls with their long faces silently stared at me from all angles. With the empty sink sprinkled with dried toothpaste crust splatters, to the extra sensitive soap smeared around and baby shampoo for my radiated scalp that fell off the tub and started to drip across the white floor, the place was inviting for someone who had to spew. I dropped on my knees next to the toilet, and my stomach automatically started heaving.

My jaw flew unnaturally wide open like the killer in *Scream*. My stomach was completely empty. My course breathing squeezed in between the dry contractions of my stomach muscles. "Huuh!" Still nothing came out. The contractions stopped…. Seconds passed… *Is it over?*

"Huuuah…" The heaves lasted until I could barely breathe. Finally, something came up; it was that horrible stomach acidy stuff that burns. My stomach was satisfied now that its involuntary spasms had finally produced something. I fell backwards with relief and hardly realized my bald head slamming against the wall with a jolt.

• • •

January, 1998

It was 7:00 in the morning, and we had to be at the hospital by 8:30. I had finished my last radiation treatment of the six-week cycle somewhere around the beginning of the 1997 Christmas season. I got to go home for Christmas and salvage what I could from my old life. I visited friends, and spent the holiday with my family.

Now I was back at St. Jude's. Today, I was going to start my first bone marrow transplant and be locked away in a hospital room for the first round of chemotherapy. I had heard so many terrible things about it - that it makes most people sick, green, and bald. I pictured a golden substance, similar to the look of tea, but poisonous like snake venom. It was circulating through my body and burning up every little bit of tissue like some sort of acid." The doctors would be like, "Well it burned all your insides away, so you're pretty much dead, but your cancer's all gone. Woop Woop!"

"JOHN CATHCART, PLEASE COME TO ASSESSMENT/TRIAGE!!! JOHN CATHCART PLEASE

COME TO ASSESSMENT/TRIAGE!" Some lady blared my name over the loud speaker like an announcer calls the starting lineup at a football game.

"43 Kg," the scale in the floor read. This is 94.6 pounds. My weight had gone down a bunch since radiation. While being radiated, I wouldn't eat much of anything. I would try to eat things I loved, like chili. I used to love Mom's chili. It was warm and satisfying, especially by the fire on a cold winter day, or during a football game. But my taste for such goodies had changed. I couldn't touch any chili when I went home that Christmas.

As the nurse wrote down my vital signs, she started shaking her head in pity. "Looks like they have a blood test for you today sweetie. You're gonna have to go to the lab…" The horrible statement echoed in my head, sending a shiver down my spine.

They wanted my blood. The entrance stuck out from a corner in the middle of a hallway just before the main waiting room. The semi-crooked and eerie sign at the door read "LAB." It wasn't really crooked, but it was to me, because it represented the purpose behind the lab: to make kids suffer. We cautiously made our way into the small room. Light blue chairs lined the walls. A parent cradling his or her terrified child occupied each one. As we came in, everyone's eyes turned to us, as if we were walking into a torture chamber and we were the next victims in line. All of the parents' faces showed sympathy. The children's shivering faces showed fear. Black, white, yellow, or brown… ethnicity didn't matter, because at that level of fear everything is the same. Features such as a child's swelling bottom lip or the shiver of their wet eyes spelled the same connotation of fear and anxiety no matter what. I grabbed a number from a dispenser hanging on a wall. Nothing was personal in the lab; it was just about taking blood from large numbers of people. They just called you by numbers like at a DMV.

Kristin, Mom and I walked down through the middle of the chairs toward the end by the second door. I could feel the sympathetic eyes of fellow blood victims follow me across the room, curious of what I did to get in there, wondering if my fate held the same weight as theirs, wondering… "Who's more hardcore, who suffers more, me or him? I bet I suffer more than him… Poor guy, he doesn't know what he's in for…" I'm sure it's what they were thinking.

While I waited either flipping through the old magazines piled on tables, or sleeping on Mom's shoulder, every once in a while I could hear the screams of children from behind the door of the LAB - children who were getting their blood vacuumed out of their little arms with sharp metal tubes driven in by strangers… or the whimpers of the kids who made the mistake of watching the needle slowly plunge into their skin. Parents were usually not allowed back in the lab because it was too crowded. So once the kids left the waiting room, they were on their own.

"Numba 42." A lady peeked through the door and called out my number. *That's it. It is time…* I stood up and gloomily faced the door. I slowly walked in, like a soldier marching off into a battle of guaranteed death. I bade farewell to Mom and Kristin at the blue chairs with a salute. I bit my tongue as I followed the smiling nurse into the lab. I knew there was an abundance of evil behind that smile, a devil leading me to the fires.

"Can you go slow please?" I asked the nurse manhandling the giant needle. At least for me, I didn't have to get stuck with a needle for blood. I used to have to back when I didn't have a line. They would stick the needle into a rubber tube that was connected to my line, and pull back on it just like they would a syringe in my arm.

They would usually yank back hard on the syringe, creating a vacuum inside that sucked blood from my chest to the tube. A lot of times when they yanked on the syringe in my line, the vein inside me sort of collapsed or tightened because there was not enough blood readily available and the syringe sucked too hard. I hated this feeling. It gave me nauseating tingles all over and I could just feel the heavy veins in my chest crumple under the pull, begging for mercy. Therefore, I always asked the nurse to pull back slowly so that it wouldn't happen. However, they never seemed to quite understand how bad it really felt, because they never really slowed down.

I stumbled out of the door like a drunk. I felt beaten and deprived of blood. Mom saw my hurt, but we had to move on. "Now to the main waiting room for your D-clinic appointment with Gajjar," she said.

Dr. Gajjar was my main doctor at St. Jude's. He was a fast-paced man from India with a kind heart, always in a hurry. He was built like Dad. He carried with him a funny black mustache and an aura of incredible intelligence. Dr. Gajjar specialized in my type of cancer. He knew everything there was to know about Medulloblastomas.

"Stem cells," Dr. Gajjar explained in his rapid dialect, "...are the early components of all body parts." Inside the clinical room, Dr. Gajjar was explaining to me what stem cells were and why I should be aware of what was happening to them during my chemo. "At the very earliest time of life when the egg with its 23 chromosomes and the sperm with 23 chromosomes come together, they make a new cell with 46 chromosomes. These chromosomes contain all of the instructions that will make up a new person... a blueprint of what they look like: the color of their hair, their eyes, blood type, and even to some degree their personality. Only a few days after the glorious union, that new cell then goes on to divide and forms a bag of cells called a blastocyst. This blastocyst eventually implants itself in the uterus and grows to become a new person. All of the cells of that new person contain the exact same chromosomes as the original cell made up from the sperm and egg coming together."

He paused to see if anything registered in me yet. I just stared wide eyed and nodded my head.

"The cells making up the bag are then called stem cells – "stem" in that all the specialized cells that come after them are *stemming* from those original cells, similar to a plant stem. True stem cells contain all of the information to make any other cell in the body. As cells continue to divide and become more specialized, they become less able to become something else. For example, it would

61

be difficult for a cell that is already almost a heart cell to become a brain cell. Even though it has the same chromosomes, it is not a stem cell anymore, and therefore it cannot differentiate itself to another cell type. Only stem cells, which have not fully declared themselves as a specific cell type yet, can do that. There are many different types of stem cells in the body. Research is actually being done on those very early stem cells in the blastocyst because they can theoretically be manually directed to become any cell type, and repair or grow a new part of the body that had been damaged. These are also sometimes referred to as embryonic stem cells. So, as cells in their early stage continue to become more specialized, many turn into blood cells. The earliest blood cells, those that can become any type of blood cell, are also referred to as stem cells in that they are the earliest offspring of all blood cells: red, white, platelets, and so on. Blood stem cells are made in the bone marrow. As they grow up, they are released into the blood stream and they turn into other types of blood cells."

"The chemotherapy drugs that we will give you, John, are strong enough to kill every cell in your body that is dividing. Blood cells are always dividing, and the chemotherapy will destroy most every blood cell in your body, and you would not survive. Therefore, before we start any chemo, we will harvest your blood stem cells, the ones that contain information to become all types of blood cells. We will take your blood stem cells from inside your bone marrow that flows inside your bones, store it in baggies, and freeze it. When you are finished with each round of chemo and it has had several days to dissipate from your body, we will pump some of your stem cells back into you so that your body can recover with fresh, new blood cells growing everywhere. Do you understand? Do you understand John...? John?"

• • •

Our next and last appointment for the day was Pulmonary Function, and that wasn't scheduled for a half an hour later. We walked back out into the waiting room, and I was greeted by the outlandish bunch of little brothers and sisters of patients who ran about making noises and throwing out headaches, and the loud families yapping in different languages. The gloomy patients and sad parents were slouched over like willow trees.

One small couch/chair was open. There was only enough room for two, so Kristin volunteered to go sit by herself. I could see the uneasiness in Mom's face as she was about to sit on the light blue cushion beside me.

In the center of all of the light blue couch/chairs, there were several games and toys for children to play with: little tables covered with paper and crayons, a cart full of hand-held video games and various board games that have been donated.

I was watching the children run around. A little Hispanic boy of about three caught my eye as he left his mom's side while she dozed off on the couch/chairs. He waddled off independently to one of the small tables. Some tables had little towns on top of them. There were several buildings, parks, and streets, a miniature community. There were magnets underneath the tables that kids could move around with their hands, and the magnets moved the cars and people inside the little towns. Each of the people had little happy faces with a simple smile and two dots for eyes. The cars had faces too.

I examined the boy's eager face as he grabbed hold of the magnets underneath. His eyes lit up when he realized that he was moving the cars and people himself; that he was in control in his little town. I watched as his smile grew, his intent eyes focusing on every move. I noticed his shunt. *This kid had a brain tumor removed recently.* Many times after a brain surgery, a child's head will constantly leak small amounts of fluid. Therefore, certain patients have a shunt put in. It's a small tube just below the skin on their heads that lets the fluid drain out. It sticks out on most bald children. It looks like a vein popping out from the arm of a body builder.

A little girl hobbled past him. She seemed about five or six, American, blond hair, blue eyes. And although there were only a few long and thin strands of hair on her head, she had a cute little pink bow on top of it. She wore a pink dress and white Keds.

63

I could see her line bundled up inside of her dress. It took up more than half of her upper body. Her smile stretched proportionally to her wide-open eyes as she looked at the magnetic table and watched the people on top magically move around. She made her way to another table in the middle of the waiting room. A long piece of paper stretched across it as a tablecloth for kids to draw on. On the other end of the table was a toddler standing in his mother's lap, scribbling on the paper with several crayons. The little girl then grabbed a crayon and started exporting her smile from mind to paper with the colored wax.

I sat in my blue chair next to Mom observing the room and thinking. A lot of people were frowning, but the majority of the smaller kids didn't have the same frown. Even though they had the same troubles, I assumed they didn't have as much to lose as the older kids who could be back at home in school with their friends. *It's almost as if some of the kids don't completely realize that what they are going through is so abnormal. They haven't really been exposed to enough life yet, and they think this is how it's supposed to be... as good as it gets. They don't know much else and are fascinated at the smallest bits of pleasure, like simple toys or crayons. Maybe something else is making them smile. This little girl is smiling...*

Time seemed to slow down, and the atmosphere around the children froze. I dozily fell into the present moment. Sometimes these "moments" happen when I look at the ocean, or mountains, or sometimes while on a run.

Silence danced around like a ballerina; the only thing I could hear was the sound of the kids with the toys laughing in slow motion and the ringing in my ears. The clicks and pencil marks of the kids writing on the tables became amplified. I experienced the sincerity of the cries from kids around the couch/chairs. The little girl had finished her masterpiece and waddled away from the table, leaving her crayons to roll off. They traveled down through the air as slowly and gracefully as a kite. They hit the floor with a loud thud and they left streak marks of blue and yellow, and the booming echo filled my ears like thunder. At this same time I looked up at the little girl's drawing.

It was silly, and I didn't know what to think. I was slightly angry and slightly jealous, because I didn't understand. I didn't smile or frown, but I kept looking at the girl as she smiled and waddled away. There were three words in sloppy, Comic Sans-esc letters, "jeSuS lOVes mE."

...

I put my hands together and bowed my head whenever I tried to pray. I did just like the butt-chinned man who seemed to pray so perfectly. *He probably got me into this whole mess in the first place; put a curse on me or something...* My battles with cancer treatment had been coming to an end. But it was stupid. I knew there was nothing there – or there was something, but some force of evil. If I were to even look at God again, He would probably cast more cancer on me, next time ending me for sure.

Despite the 20 or so cards I unwrapped every day during treatment that told me "God holds you in His hands," and "You're so lucky to have God," *I never saw God put me in anyone's hands or even hold my own while I was on the operating tables or the exam room beds, sizzling from beams of radiation. I never saw any footprints in the sand.* I had felt like an object of entertainment. *Does God enjoy watching me fry, like a helpless roach lit aflame by some curious pyrotechnic kid who stares and laughs as they squirm?* Despite the churches all across the country that said they had put me on their "prayer lists," and the thousands of prayers from people I have never or will never see in my life, I obviously wasn't getting stronger or healthier with each prayer.

5
The Cider House

March 1998

Well, no patient at St. Jude's Hospital became close friends with one another. It seemed that maybe because everyone was too sick to be friendly. Most patients were babies or little kids who were too shy to talk to anyone but their parents. I was a preteen and, in addition to the pangs of treatment, loneliness, and helplessness, I was driven mad every day by the whining little kids. Every moment I thought about what was going on back at home with my friends.

In order to ease my time at St. Jude, I was visited frequently by the child-life-specialist, Mark. His job was to make sure everyone at St. Jude's had a friend. Mark would see me in the waiting rooms sometimes. He'd come sit and joke like any friend would. He would always come up to me with excitement and tell me about something going on around the hospital like drawing contests, celebrity visitors, free giveaways, fun things like that.

"What's up Johnny?" he would say when he was just saying hi. He was always extremely busy. Whenever he could be seen, he was frantically running around, trying to be a friend to all the friend-needy kids at St. Jude's. He did a great job.

It was some time after my first round of chemotherapy when Mark sat next to me while I was sitting in a noisy room, waiting to be called for a D-Clinic appointment. "Hey Johnny," he said. "You know, I found these people that do cool things for kids in the hospital just like you. These people are like genies. They'll take you anywhere in the world for free, even to places like Disneyland. Here." He handed me this colorful piece of paper. "Take a look." I looked around the paper from color to color, getting lost in all the little smiley faces sappily tucked away in fluffy clouds and rainbows. My eyes came upon the bold-faced title across the top. "Make-A-Wish Foundation." *Hmmmmmm…* I read on. It said something like this.

Welcome to the Make-a-Wish Foundation! We are here to make your battle with disease more comfortable. Have you ever wanted a genie to come and grant your wish? We are a group of genies. If you have a wish to go anywhere, meet anyone, or see anything in the world, then we will grant that wish. Just write back telling us about your wildest dream, and we'll do our absolute best to see that your dream comes true! Meanwhile, keep up the good fight!
-Sincerely,
The Genies at Make-A-Wish Foundation

"What do you think?" Mark asked.

· · ·

I came home from Tennessee about the same time the seventh grade got out. I missed out on the entire year, but at least I passed by doing all the lessons and homework on my own woozy time while I was getting treated.

I had the whole summer after that to relax and recover in order to start the eighth grade as a mostly normal kid. Mom and I decided that I would wait until I got done with treatment to write the Make-A-Wish Foundation about my wish. It wouldn't have made sense to go to Disneyland or on a vacation to some foreign country while I was sick, skinny and bald. So we thought the summer I had to recover would be perfect. All summer I was still sick, skinny, and bald because it took forever to recover from a year of cancer treatment. However, it wasn't long until I was at least in excellent condition to make a wish.

My wish was obvious. I loved movies and I wanted to be a part of one. The usual wish is to go to Disneyland or to meet some celebrity, so I wasn't sure if this one was going to fly. My wish was short and simply stated, although probably not very simple to grant. I wrote to the genies at the Make-A-Wish Foundation a few days after I got home. This is my letter. I was thirteen.

Dear Make-A-Wish Foundation, My name is Johnny Cathcart. I was treated for cancer at St. Jude's Children's Research Hospital for the past year. I am done with cancer now, and I have a wish. I love movies, and I wish to somehow be involved in a major motion picture. I want to be on set, and meet the people who make it. That is all. I hope you can grant my wish.
Thank you,
John Cathcart

The whole summer passed and I did not hear back from the Make-A-Wish Foundation. The eighth grade came on heavy with a lot of work and a lot of social pressure. I had grown a few hairs on top of my head, but I was mostly still bald from my treatments. It looked like one of those military crew cuts because I had short dark hair just on the top.

Everyone knew what had happened to me, so everyone was quick to be my friend, even the teachers. I instantly became one of the most popular kids in school when I first walked in the door that year.

About two months of school passed before I did finally get a letter back from the Make-A-Wish Foundation. It said they were sorry for taking so long. It took them a while because my wish was the first of its kind. What I wanted was a little out of the ballpark from what they normally do. But fortunately, the hearts of the Make-A-Wish volunteers assigned to grant my wish were a little out of the ballpark as well.

They stuck to my wish and not only granted it, but found me a part in a big-budget movie from Miramax Films and director Lasse Hallstrom. Make-A-wish contacted actor Paul Rudd whose parents lived in Kansas City, close to my hometown of St. Joe. Paul found a perfect spot for me to play in the current movie he was working on, *The Cider House Rules*, a film based on a novel by John Irving. The film is heavily centered around an orphanage, with some of the kids being very sick. I was perfect for the part.

The two people at Make-A-Wish set everything up wonderfully. The large envelope I got in the mail from them enclosed three round-trip airline tickets to North Hampton, Massachusetts in a month. That was where the movie was currently being filmed. The envelope held an order form for pictures and $100 to buy them with. The letter inside said that the movie people wanted to see some black and white photos of me. It was hard for me to believe what I was reading. *How exciting! A movie director wants pictures of me!* In the letter was also the name of a hotel where they had already booked my parents and I a room. This hotel was supposed to be where most of the cast and crew were staying.

Something else was inside the envelope. It was a bundle of stapled papers. On the front cover page was a title: *The Cider House Rules, Adapted from the novel by John Irving. It's the script!!!* I was getting more and more excited by the second. I flipped through the pages. It was all written out just like a play. There were the names of the characters and then lines for each of them to say. Blocking directions were before and after the speaking parts, telling the actors where and how to move about just like they were on a stage. It started out with a monologue from the first character, Dr. Larch.

FADE IN: EXT. ST. CLOUD'S TRAIN STATION – DAWN

Establishing shot of the run-down train station. It is dawn on an overcast morning.

<u>*Dr. Larch*</u>
In other parts of the world young men of promise leave home to make their fortunes,
battle evil, or solve the problems of the world.

Behind the station, a boarded up paper mill stands as the only evidence of the long-gone community.
At the top of the hill lies the St. Cloud's orphanage.

<u>*Dr. Larch*</u>
I was, myself, such a young man
when I came to save the orphanage in the
abandoned logging town of St. Cloud's many years ago…

This is what the first page of the script looked like. It was amazing. It was the bones of what I had seen on the big screens all my life. It was the back stage. It was the inside that none of the public ever got to see.

I finished the script that night. In a nutshell, *Cider House Rules* is about a boy named Homer Wells who grows up in an orphanage. Since Homer was never adopted, the orphanage became his home, and Dr. Larch, the head physician at the orphanage, more or less becomes his father. Dr. Larch wants Homer to become a doctor in the orphanage just like himself. Dr. Larch performs abortions for people who either don't want or can't afford their children. Some babies are dropped off at the doorsteps of the orphanage just like a daily newspaper. Thus, Dr. Larch has no choice but to raise these children. Homer grows up feeling stuck. He wants to get out and see the world. He soon finds his ticket out with a young couple that comes for an abortion. Homer finds a new life out in the country, but in the end he comes back to the orphanage and eventually takes Dr. Larch's place after he dies.

It was amazing to me. The script spelled out camera movements and facial expressions. It wasn't like reading a book. It was like reading a movie. Picture a movie script like this: If you were blind and watched a movie sitting next to an artistic friend, then every detailed description you would hear from that friend throughout the whole film would be just like a script.

· · ·

August 1998

I kept quiet at school the next day. My jolly attitude attracted little attention. I was a soon-to-be movie star amidst a sea of amateurs. I felt like a criminal holding back important information all day. I didn't want the word to get out. I guess I was a little selfish by not telling anyone, but I would have felt uncomfortable if everyone knew.

The time came when I was to leave for Massachusetts, and the word inevitably got out. When we left, Mom had a letter sent to the principal explaining why I would be gone for two weeks.

When the principal read the note, "John is going to be absent this next week because he is filming a movie," I wondered what everyone in the office thought when he fell on the ground laughing hysterically. The office sent all of the absent report notes to the teachers. Unfortunately, when my algebra teacher got it, she read it aloud word-for-word in front of class. "…John is off making a movie… Thank you." When she got done, she realized at the top of the note it said, "PLEASE DO NOT READ OUT LOUD."

I really didn't want anyone to know. I felt like people would get the message that I got there just because I had cancer and I was "special." I didn't want people to think I was special; I just wanted to be normal. But how can you still be normal when you're a bald thirteen year old acting in an Hollywood movie while fighting cancer.

• • •

We exited the plane at North Hampton, Massachusetts and walked the long airy elevated hallway into the airport. Two anxious-looking young ladies eyed us from the terminal inside. One of them held up a white sign that said, "Make-A-Wish Foundation." Eventually we made eye contact. They were the two ladies who helped put my wish together. They smiled and came over to us. They introduced themselves and handed Mom a huge bouquet of flowers like she had just sang an opera. They hugged us like people who hadn't seen each other for years, and said they were going to "Escort me to the big show."

One of the ladies handed me a trip itinerary. It had directions to where we would be going, our room number at the hotel, a map to the set, and the time when we were supposed to appear. The other one then handed me an envelope with $500 in it. "That's spending-money for you; it's from the Make-A-Wish Foundation. Use it to go out to eat and get some fun souvenirs for yourself. Now, let's go make you a star!"

$500! I couldn't believe it. It all seemed to happen so fast. The ladies were like angels that fell from the sky. Their mission was to make sure I was as happy as I could be. They led us through the terminal and didn't ever stop letting us know how excited they were to do this for me. They brought us out of the airport doors and pointed us to a shiny black stretch limo waiting for me in the drive. They hugged us like we would never see each other again, and waved us off as we rolled away.

The limo dropped us off at this hotel seemingly out in the middle of nowhere. Make-A-Wish had arranged a rental car to be left for us out in the parking lot, and we pulled up next to it. The hotel was a good size; just one story high, but it all circled around this enormous glass dome that was about half a football field wide and half a football field tall. It looked like a giant car from *The Jetsons*.

The overwhelming awesomeness of the situation would not allow the full smile to leave my face. It was frozen on me like a clown. We waved goodbye to the limo driver like we did the ladies who had graciously assisted us on our journey, and turned to walk into my future.

• • •

We settled into the hotel that night, and at 9:00 the next morning, we left in the new rental car and followed our map to the set.

The Massachusetts countryside was beautiful. With the tall grass swaying in the wind and the lone trees's silhouettes sort of dancing in the morning sun, the landscape was like a moving painting. After five minutes or so, we came to what looked like an old, small, abandoned college campus back on a hill off a gravel road. I noticed people busily moving about inside. *It's the Cider House Rules…* There were people running around everywhere, each with important jobs like in an ant colony. We drove closer. It was amazing how this place seemed so far out away from everything, but then all of this was going on in this secluded area.

It was like a little lost civilization, or a traveling circus community setting up for a show. We parked and walked up to the commotion in the busy village.

We hiked closer and closer into the campus, and stopped at the first dark wooden building on a hill. It looked like it was about to fall apart. We stopped because we noticed a woman walking down the side on a set of creaky steps. She was dressed normally in blue jeans and an autumn-style orange shirt with a plaid bandana upon her head. She glanced in our direction then stopped, turned, and waited for the strangers she saw to approach. "Can I help you?" she called out. We finally came within talking distance, and Mom responded in a delightful professional tone as to ensure in this lady's mind that we were indeed there on real official business.

"Hi, we are from the Make-A-Wish Foundation and we're here to…"

The lady cut her off. "Well then, you must be Mr. Joooohn Cathcart!" I nodded, very proud to be recognized by someone on the movie set. "Well, welcome aboard! My name is Laura McDonald. I'm one of the head costume designers for the movie here. They told me to be lookin' out for yah and to help find you a good-lookin' costume first thing!" My parents happily shook hands and introduced themselves. We were relieved that we had found someone that knew what was going on; and this lady was more than helpful.

"… Great! Well, let's get to it, shall we? C'mon, follow me up the stairs to the wardrobe and I'll get you suited all up to look like a little orphan! You'll fit right in with the rest." *Wow, we're not wasting any time.* That was supposedly my role, an orphan. We followed her back up the wooden steps into the shaggy old building that looked like it was once a church. Inside, it was just one huge room like a giant attic. It was filled with multiple rows of long clotheslines crammed with hundreds of hangers and old-style clothing that you would see on every class of characters in *Titanic.*

I stepped up to the first row. There were all sorts of shapes and sizes of old raggedy pants. I took off a brown pair of slacks and sized them up to myself. They were for some hefty guy. *But wait... These pants are not just for any hefty guy. Jeez, they could have been worn by... John Candy, or Danny Devito!* I imagined that I had probably seen this same pair of pants before on the big screen at some point in my life. The thoughts were just all too exciting.

"If you'd just mosey on over here, I'll measure you up for some clothes!" Laura the costume lady called out. I walked over, and she started going all around me with a tape measure just like they do when you're getting measured for a prom tuxedo. "So, where yah from?" she asked. "Oh, from St. Joseph, Missouri..." She went on measuring around asking me small-talk questions like a conversation with a barber. I loved it when someone measured all around me like Laura was doing. It sent this tranquil buzz down my neck – close to the feeling back in elementary school when the mothers would line up and go through each kid's hair searching for lice with little wooden sticks. That was the greatest feeling. Although I never actually had lice, I'd say to them... "I think there's some crawling around right here... and maybe here."

She found me a pair of brown pants, a gray V-neck shirt with collars that stuck out, and suspenders that all fit so well I looked dorky. "Hmm... You look great, but there's one thing missing..." She said. Then she pulled out this little fisherman's hat and propped it up on my head. "Perfect!"

Laura stood back and happily clasped her hands together. "Alright! I'm going to be off now. To be honest, I don't know where they want you next, but if you'll just walk that way, you should find someone who does. Most everyone knows that you are coming, so just tell them your name. Good luck!" Laura had pointed us toward the middle of the campus.

We waved to her as we stepped down a different staircase along the other side of the building. We walked further into the community to take on our next task. We were walking among other people now. We didn't exactly look like we knew what we were doing. People having conversations with their headsets hurriedly passed by, giving us these accusing looks that made us feel in the way like tourists in New York. One woman eyed us from under an umbrella next to a mobile bar. Painted on the side of the bar was: *TONY'S FINE MOTION PICTURE CATERING.* The woman was walking up to us.

"Are you John Cathcart?" she asked.

Dad answered for me, "Yes, we're with the Make-A-Wish Foundation and…"

She cut him off with an inviting Southern bell voice, "Well, I am so glad to meet ya'll! My name is Brenda McNally. I'm one of the hair designers around here. I've heard all about you and your wish to come here and be with us. Welcome!" My parents introduced themselves. She talked on. "Is there anything I can help you with, get you some food, show you around, or maybe help you find your way?"

Brenda delightfully volunteered to give us a tour of the set. We followed her around, and she told us everything. She would often run into people and say something like "Hey so-and-so, this is John Cathcart!" She was excited to show me off. The first place she pointed at was the bar on wheels I had seen a minute ago. "This is the place that you can come and get all of your snacks and goodies. Speaking of food, we get to eat lunch in about an hour or so, and that's the cafeteria over there." She pointed to the bottom of a stout brick building. Down the hill and to the left were two lines of about four or five big campers.

"What are those for?" I asked.

"Those are trailers where some of the cast and crew stay during the filming. Here, I'll come show yah." She explained as we walked. "These trailers are for all of the main characters like Wally, Dr. Larch, some of the more important orphans, and other people like that. They even have a trailer all set up for you I hear! V.I.P. treatment!" *My own trailer!?*

She walked me down between the rows of trailers and told me about the people staying there. "This here is Paul Rudd's trailer. In *The Cider House Rules* he plays the soldier, Wally. You might remember him from the movie *Clueless.* This one here is Charlize

Theron's trailer. She plays the girlfriend of Wally, and she's been in this... and that and..." She just counted them off one by one like it was no big news to her. It was like she was doing roll call. "The next trailer is Michael Caine's. He plays Dr. Larch. He's been in movies ever since I was a little kid. Next is Toby Maguire's. This young man has done this... and that..." Everything she was saying was just too much for me at the moment. Her voice faded in and out.

"Where's the trailer they have for me?" I asked. "Well actually, it's this one right here." "Cool!" There were two doors, one on either end. I asked why. She said that the trailer was divided in half like a duplex. "Kieran Culkin is staying on the right side. And you are on the left," she said. *Woa! Kieran Culkin! Sharing a trailer with me?*

Brenda opened my door and I walked in. Inside, it was normal and clean - just like a nice hotel room with beds, a TV, and a bathroom. " Now lunch starts in 30 minutes. You can wait here until then, or walk around and meet more people if you'd like. See yah at lunch!" We thanked her and waved goodbye. My parents and I were soaking up all that just happened, and time flew by. Before we knew it, it was time for lunch.

Inside the cafeteria, there was a huge line of interesting-looking people (most still in costume) walking slowly through a long bar with all sorts of food. It was just like a school cafeteria. It was amazing for me to see these things happen. It was the movies, the big time, but everything was normal, just like an everyday food place. It was all so... unexpected.

We stood in line just looking around at the different people in amazement, wondering who they might be or what they might do. We got our food, which was surprisingly normal as well. I thought it would be gourmet gold-sprinkled or something. Once Mom, Dad, and I had some good-looking corn dogs on our plates, we all suddenly became very vulnerable. The question was, "Where to sit?"

We just stood there sheepishly looking around like kids at a new school. A young guy with short and curly black hair smiled at us from a table nearby. He motioned us over to sit next to him. I was kind of nervous. *Maybe he had us mistaken for someone else; some other movie star...* "You must be John Cathcart?" he said.

"That's me!" I claimed.

He replied, "My name is Paul. I play Wally in the movie." At that moment I recognized him. It was the guy who played Josh in the movie *Clueless.* "Make-A-Wish called my parents," Paul said.

"And I'm Toby," said the younger guy on the other side of the table. He looked like he was about 18 or 19.

I greeted the two, beat my dad to introducing ourselves, and sat down next to them with my tray of corndogs. I don't know how, but after a little small-talk, we broke into this normal conversation about dogs in movies. I was surprised at how friendly these people were. It was just like everyday lunchtime at school. I sat with Paul and Toby for the rest of the time. Throughout the conversation, I became a little upset with myself for being so excited, like I didn't expect them to be as real as they were, and I felt stupid, yet relieved. They were all just average folks who were happy with their corndogs.

When I went back to my trailer after lunch, I took a long look in the mirror. There was myself, and the movie set in the back window. I fell back on the bed that had been made up for me by some movie star maid. I looked at the costume on my body and felt through the cottons and wools that must have been worn in all sorts of movies before. The excitement of the moment overtook me as I realized my life must have been taking me somewhere.

· · ·

The hotel was very nice. Under a giant dome in the middle, all the rooms were circled around a big orange-tiled courtyard area. We could see all the other rooms from ours, and everyone could just walk right out into a big common area. There was a nice warm pool, arcade games, and a big hot tub. Most everyone staying there was working on the movie. People like Paul or Toby didn't stay there, but all of the orphans did including Kieran. After working on the movie all day, everyone would come back to the hotel and relax in the pool and hot tub together.

I hung out with Kieran and this small kid named Eric, the little brother in *Malcolm in the Middle,* and several other orphans from the film. Most of them were younger than I was, except Kieran who was a year older, but we all had a good time in the pool running around and stuff just like anybody would. We sat in the hot tub a lot. The whole time I was still baffled by the people I was with. Before then, movie people had just been these sort of mythological creatures to me, in a another realm guarded heavily by an army of Oprah Security guards. But every moment I spent with them, I became more and more aware of how human they were. They were just here doing their job.

• • •

The next day I got to work in front of the camera. In the morning, we drove right to my trailer where I changed into my orphan outfit, and this nervous young guy I hadn't seen before knocked on our door. He was tall, skinny, and wore a black baseball cap. "I'm the second assistant director," he said. He told me that they were to shoot my scene in nearly four hours, but that I was welcome to come watch the shot they were currently working on. Mom, Dad, and I followed the jittery young man through the set to the building where they were shooting.

When you watch the movie, it looks like most of the story takes place in one big orphanage building. I walked by several old abandoned buildings around the set that were being used for different shots. In one of the last buildings on campus before some fields, we followed the guy up to the third floor hallway to a room at the end and into the corner of another room to find the movie crew through a doorway in that corner. Other parts of the orphanage were all filmed in different buildings that look like one big place in the movie. A lot of it was even filmed in different states. Learning about this made me feel like I'd been tricked all of my life.

As I approached the set, I lost myself in the mob of people in the hallway, all running around yapping, looking like they knew what they were doing. There was a table full of snacks and hors d'oeuvres up to my left where some of the kids, dressed like orphans, were impishly stuffing their faces. There were some normally dressed people sitting around a table in one of the rooms off the hallway. They were busily discussing something that required their hands to thrust up and down. Straight through the crowd of people in front of me was the man behind the camera.

The camera was gigantic, with all sorts of high-tech looking attachments. A casually dressed, older European man sat behind it giving orders to some people in front. His chair sat on wheels that were situated on what looked like a short set of train tracks. *He must be the director...* I noticed that there was some sort of smoke coming from two pipes around the actor's area in front of the camera. However, it wasn't gray smoke: it was clear like steam. It made the whole area look soft like the movie screen does. *So that's how they do it...*

The nervous second assistant director had already run away from us, so we felt a little out of place just standing around again. Paul Rudd was one of the people in front of the camera. So despite our feeling of not belonging, at least we knew someone important there. Paul noticed us out of the corner of his eye and immediately walked over to us.

"Hey buddy... How's it going?"

"Excellent," I said.

"Here, I want you to come meet the director." He took my hand and brought me to the director giving orders from behind the camera. I was getting nervous walking up to him. He was like a king on a throne. I was just some insignificant townsfolk being escorted to him by a Jester. I would have to bow and kiss his feet. We appeared in his sight and he turned to us. His serious order-giving face turned into a smile when he saw me, like when King Mufasa smiles at Zazoo in the opening scene to the Lion King.

"Hey Paul, what's up?" he asked. Paul chatted with him for a second and then introduced me and my parents. "This is John Cathcart, the boy I told you about from the Make-A-Wish Foundation." The tall king descended from his throne and shook my hand with an experienced, firm grip.

He spoke with a deep Swedish accent. "Why hello young man! I'm Lasse. I've heard quite a lot about you, and I'm proud to have you here working with us!" *Working with us? Proud? He's heard about me? This is unbelievable…*

"Can you hang on just one second?" he asked.

"Sure." I said. We waited a minute while Lasse finished giving some orders and told the actors to take a break. He turned back to me and talked for a minute about why I was here and what I would be doing.

"So you like the movies, huh?" he asked. He showed me the camera and the set in front of it. He told me about the smoke, the train track, the artificial frost on the windows, and even the snack table. "So for now, you can either hang around here and watch, or you can go chill in your trailer and wait for whenever we need you. It will probably be a couple of hours and then we will send someone to come find you. Just stay around set somewhere, and have yourself some fun," he added as he was getting up.

"Excuse me for now, cause *I* need to find something to snack on myself."

Paul, patiently observing our conversation from along side, said, "I better go also. I need to get ready."

"Nice to meet you Johnny!" Lasse said. *He called me Johnny…* I'm not really sure why, maybe it just has a more characterized ring to it, but it ignites a warm feeling in me when people who only know me as John call me Johnny.

We spent about ten minutes just bouncing our eyes from one thing to the next: all the expensive-looking monitors, computers, microphones, and lights - there were so many extremely bright lights. It was hard to look into them, not only because they were so bright, but also because they were hot like the sun.

Several people came up and introduced themselves to us. We met people such as Jane Alexander and Cathy Baker, who played the two nurses in the movie. Also, some of the orphans came up to me and talked. They asked if I wanted to play laser-tag with them later.

After about 20 minutes of noise, everything seemed to calm down. We watched as this beautiful woman walked in along with Paul Rudd. She was tall with short blond hair, eyebrows thin and crisp arched stunningly over her shiny eyes. She had skin that looked like it was woven of a kind of silk. They followed Lasse, and after a few minutes of people getting situated all around, someone yelled, "Quiet on the set!" There was an immediate dead silence. It was like someone hit the mute button. Lasse stood aside from the camera and there was some other man on it now.

Paul and the woman walked behind a door. Smoke rose throughout the hall. Lights dimmed and focused on huge, white reflecting pads that angled softer light to other parts of the hall. There was a series of commands from different people. "Camera ready? – Sound ready? – Roll sound!" "Sound speeding!" They shouted them as if they were giving military roll call. "Slate!" another guy in jeans and a black shirt and hat said as he stepped out in front of the camera with a sort of clip board in his hands. It had some writing on it. The top was a bar with big orange and black stripes. He didn't look like an actor. "Cider House, shot 12:d, take one!" he announced like a football referee. "Camera speed!" someone else yelled. The man in the black hat lifted the top off his little board and snapped it back down making a loud crack. It seemed like I was hearing all the wrong things. I wasn't hearing what I expected. *Speed..? The speed of the film? The speed of the people moving on the camera?* But finally I recognized something.

"Action!" Lasse Hallstrom commanded.

This is it! My mind was racing with excitement. *This is what people will see on big screens all across the world.* It was definitely exciting to be a part of and watch it all take place before my own eyes. The tension plateaued as nurse (Cathy) slowly walked out of a door adjacent the hallway. The camera pointed right at her. She pushed a hospital bed with the beautiful woman on it. The woman looked tired and hurt. Paul ran in from the other side of the hallway and gently grasped the woman's hand. "How's she doing?" He asked in a low and worried voice. The nurse slowly replied, "Oh fine, just fine." The silence remained as they slowly walked out of the camera's sight. "Cut!" Lasse shouted.

It was over! It was a whole eight seconds. I was ready to see them shoot the next scene. There was some mumbling among some people with headphones. After Lasse finished talking with Paul, the nurse, and the beautiful girl, they went away again. The next scene was coming up. The lights adjusted, the silence kicked in once again, and the man in the black hat came out to clap his board. Lasse yelled "Action!"

The same nurse walked out pushing the same bed with the same tired and beautiful woman. Paul ran out again, "How's she doing?" he said. "Oh fine, just fine." They slowly walked out of the camera's view.

It was the same thing... Nothing seemed different. I did some quick wondering. I just sat and watched as they all talked and got ready to do another one. It was the same thing again. They did it again, and again, and again, and again, and again. There were about 10 takes of that one shot. I didn't notice that Toby was in there too. He was standing next to me, and, noticing my unrest at the never-ending shot, he leaned in and told me that every shot was like that. He told me that every second I would see in a movie equals about an hour of work. *This is incredible!*

•••

I was startled from a little snooze in my trailer by some loud knocks on my door. It had been about an hour since I watched them shoot, and I was expecting them to come find me in another two hours or so. It was three of the other orphans with guns. One of them was Eric. They handed me a gun and a small vest that detects the lasers. "Wanna play?"

I followed them out the door and they quickly dispersed in separate directions. They ran behind parked cars and trailers to hide from each other. I strapped the vest on and readied my gun. The really cool thing is that we were all in costume. After a few minutes of quietly stalking behind some cars, we popped out into the open and unloaded on each other. I ran and tumbled with my gun like James Bond. One of the orphans jumped from behind a truck, caught me by surprise, and nailed me with the laser. My pack lit up and I jerked back suddenly like I'd just been pierced by a bullet. With the last ounce of life in me I shot my shooter down before he killed again.

We had run around the set shooting lasers for about 30 minutes, then we all decided to go sneak up on someone. "Let's go get Toby!" One of them shouted.

We tiptoed up to where Toby's trailer was. He must have been napping as well, because his light was off but the TV was blinking silently. One of them knocked as the rest of us hid underneath the steps going up to the door. In a few seconds, he walked out. "Helloooo?" The three boys simultaneously pounced on him, blasting him with lasers. I hesitated a second, but I quickly jumped in. All four of us wrestled to pin him down and we assassinated him. He moaned and vividly died in front of us. We looked down at him in victory, as he lay lifeless. He suddenly lunged up with a roar, grabbed my gun, and began shooting at us! We died and fell on top of him so he couldn't move.

Then the nervous man with the black hat popped in the door and announced, "We're ready for you guys." Nowadays I like to tell people I wrestled with Spider Man once. The makeup lady made a stop by each one of us and poked around our faces with this poofy, powdery thing. We were to go on camera in about ten minutes. The set was inside of a different old building on the campus that looked as if it were going to collapse like the others. Inside was an old dining hall where we were to be eating breakfast. It was supposed to be the cafeteria for the orphanage.

The room was large and airy with high ceilings. The oak tables were long and thin, and there were about ten in the room, all filled with kids. I sat next to one of the little girls that stayed at my hotel. Her name was Skye. She was a cute little girl, and she had those cheeks that seem to yearn for pinching. The scene we were about to shoot is ten minutes into the movie and it takes place in the morning. It is where a young couple comes to the orphanage and shops for children to adopt. All of the kids desperately want to be adopted by the couple. The orphans grow up knowing nothing outside the orphanage and would give anything to be a normal child with a real family. Therefore, whenever a couple comes, all of the kids get really excited. They would try extra hard to be cute and special, or "the best one" they would say. There are about 25 kids in the scene having pancakes and milk, and the luckiest and cutest orphan the couple picks happens to be Skye.

They had a large supply of pancakes and milk ready for us to use during the many takes of the shot. The camera was set up on more train tracks and everything was in place: the monitors, the vivid smoke, the artificial frost... Lasse was standing aside the camera talking to the cameraman. People stood all around watching, including Mom, Dad, Paul, and Toby. They were there to observe my performance debut. I wasn't supposed to say anything, just look at the camera as it came by and smile big like I was trying to look cute and get myself adopted. It took a while for everyone to get situated. Several kids had eaten their pancakes already and needed more. "Quiet on set!" someone yelled. Silence came over in a wave. They did the calls. "Action!" The film started rolling. I dug into my pancakes.

The camera, which was supposed to be the couple looking down at us, started at the far end of my table. It was going to slowly come toward me, stopping at each kid, then me, and then Skye. I thought that I would be more nervous than I was, but it was easy to get around that because the pancakes and milk were so good. *If I just act natural and enjoy the food, then I'll look excellent on camera!*

My mind raced. Whatever facial expression I decided to work up for the next couple seconds would eventually be seen by millions of people around the world. I practiced my best "cute" smile many times the previous night, and I was ready to perform. The camera came closer to me. Anticipation was building up. I just tried to enjoy my pancakes. The camera was set up at a high angle looking down at us as if it were the adopting couple. It stopped at each orphan as one of the nurses from the orphanage would say our names and briefly describe us. The tension built up inside as the camera finally turned on me. I had thought about it so much that my mind went blank. My body involuntarily slowly raised its neck and smiled its lips as big as they could get. I could feel the pancake shards stuck in my teeth, but I wasn't about to lick them clean on camera. For about four seconds the camera was on me and me alone. "And this is John, a very nice young man," the nurse said. In the movie, my face is as big as the screen for a good two seconds. The camera finally started to leave me and moved on to Skye. Lasse goes, "Cut, let's try it again."

We ran through the scene about six different times. I enjoyed a lot of pancakes. Ultimately, I must have devoured about eight of them with four large glasses of milk.

Afterward, Paul, Toby, and my parents congratulated me on my great acting job. All I did was smile, but it involved so much more! I got to take an hour break before my next scene.

It was one room down in the hallway of the same building. It was set up like a tiny old movie theatre. In the story, all of the orphans come together once a month and watch *King Kong*, the only movie they had ever seen. This time the camera wasn't on a track, just an oversized tripod beside the screen we were to watch. The room was dark. Not all the same people as before could fit into the room, just us orphans, Lasse, and a few of his henchmen. I was in the third row towards the corner of the room. In the movie, I am kind of hard to make out, but I'm there.

The camera rolled. We sat tensely on our seats watching in awe of the giant beast. *King Kong* is the best movie ever to us, and we are amazed every month when we watch it. Suddenly, the film breaks inside the projector. The orphans get upset and erupt in protest. Everyone starts banging their fists and angrily chanting, "KONG! KONG! KONG! KONG!" As I sat there banging my fists, watching the camera pan across us kids, I could feel the eyes watching me on the big screen as I yelled. It felt so good, to be a part of something that would have such an impact on so many people.

I must have certainly been there for some reason. It felt so right. I think the Make-A-Wish Foundation was just part of a bigger picture… perhaps bigger than I could wish for.

6
Coach Calls

June, 1999

"BLLLLIIIING... BLLLLIIIING!" The phone rings. A calm
Texasish yet toneless voice introduced itself to me, "Hello is this
John?" Not having ever heard a more dull yet kind voice before,
maybe on *Mr. Rogers*, I answered with much politeness and
curiosity.

"Yes this is he." I said.

"This is Coach Tom O'Brien from the Central High Cross-
Country team. I saw that you ran in the eighth grade. I'm calling
to offer you a chance to join the squad this fall." I was awestruck;
I thought immediately about my not so good physical status.
"Cross-Country? Umm... I don't know... I recently... I don't
think that I can... really..." "Oh don't worry," the voice said. "I
know all about what you've been through. I'll take good care of
you. Cross-Country is just a good opportunity to make friends,
have a good time, and get ready for high school life."

My pause told him I wasn't sure. "I'll tell you what," he said. "You
can have time to think about it, and if you want, then you can
show up for practice at the college at 6 PM on the first Monday in
August. Hopefully I'll see you there!" The college sits on the edge
of town. I showed up on that first Monday in August. I wore my
trusty blue nylon shorts and a small sleeveless shirt that brightly
displayed my puny, hairless arms. My thin blond hair flapped in
the calm breeze over my squinted blue eyes. I walked up the
gravel road to the group of young and brave athletes that
received the same inviting phone call from Coach. They all stood
in the parking lot that sat next to a long walking trail through the
woods on the campus of Missouri Western State College (now
MWSU). The trail gracefully looped around ponds and dipped
into bouquets of green trees, and then disappeared over the

wooded hills. I walked over to the other kids and instantly began sizing myself up.

I stood about 5"5". The year of cancer treatment severely stunted my growth. *At least I'm the same size as a lot of girls...* I only recognized a few people from middle school. All of the guys were taller than me. I saw my friend Gilleland from Bode. I went to stand by him. Both of us were pretty short, but he was still a little taller. All of us fresh, pre-high school kids stood around in the parking lot nervously switching our weight from foot to foot waiting for Tom O'Brien, the mysterious voice from the phone, to say something. I assumed he was the guy who stood to the side studying a clipboard. He was dressed in blue nylon shorts a good deal shorter than mine, with a blue and white Central High School Cross-Country shirt on. Short and nicely groomed dark hair covered his head.

As we waited for him to say something, I looked around at some of the girls, all of them looking good. I definitely wasn't shy. I walked up to most of the girls and introduced myself. "Hey, I'm Johnny. How's it goin'?" Most everyone was pretty friendly and happy to introduce themselves back. Once everyone's ice-breaking conversations warmed up, a loud, toneless, Southern voice interrupted them and silenced us all. It was Coach Tom O'Brien.

"He speaks." Someone whispered. In his loud monotone voice Coach shouted, "OK, let's get started! For all you newcomers, I'd like to welcome you to Central Cross-Country. You've chosen a great sport to pursue; its one of the toughest and most rewarding sports there is. Despite anyone's former thoughts about running being an individual effort, cross-country is actually very much a team sport. We practice as a team, sweat as a team, cry as a team, laugh as a team, and we win as a team. And yes, we do win. Cross-country is the most winning sport at Central High School. We are currently placed in one of the toughest districts in Missouri, and we usually win it. We come in first or second in almost every race we run, both men and women. Almost every year we have All-State runners. Every year is successful.

However, every year does not come, unless we work *our* skinny butts off, as a team. I forewarn you newcomers: for the first couple of weeks, you will go home every day tired and sore. There will be numerous times when you will do anything to make the pain stop. At first you will probably hate me. However, I guarantee you, that once you've done it, you will want to make yourself get up and do it again - each and every day. If you think you want to quit, you don't think you can handle it, then you come to me, and tell me. I'll probably tell you to run it out." His voice became almost dramatic. "But if you want to experience the indescribable, emotion-bending, breath-taking sensation of running and tackling the opponent within you, then keep it in your head until you cross that finish line."

Hm... It sounds a little tougher than what he described over the phone. He seems friendly enough though... All of the freshman stared in awe. The upperclassmen were barely paying attention because they apparently have heard this talk before.

Coach allowed us a few seconds to swallow his words. Then we listened as he lightened up a little and talked a while about what was important when running cross-country. He told us about good shoes, good eating habits (no pop, minimum fats), good mental habits, and good self-control. He handed us a number of forms to fill out: permission slips for meets and multiple health forms for our parents to sign. He also handed us a small booklet of the team's past accomplishments.

I looked through it and saw that the team was just as successful as Coach explained, and feared throughout the state of Missouri by other schools. In sports, schools are placed in different districts based on size: 1-A to 5-A. Central was a 4-A ranked school, though Central Cross-Country would compete and succeed in 5-A competitions. I read about all of the races Central won. Then I came across a training guide in the back. It gave different goals to reach and then told us how to reach them. For example, if we wanted to become a varsity team member, then it was ideal for us to run a timed mile in close to five minutes and run around eight miles a day. If we wanted to be come all-state, then it was ideal for us to run a timed mile under five minutes and run around eleven miles a day. It was ridiculous! *Who in the world would run that much?* I couldn't believe it. I looked around at some of the worried faces that were reading the same thing. *What am I getting myself into?"*

It's important to get about 15 minutes of stretching before and after practice. It's even more important to stretch after. This keeps muscles from tightening up, and prevents injuries," Coach said. The first thing we did was about 15 minutes of organized stretching, spending nearly 30 seconds on each stretch. The team formed a big circle with the senior team members gathered in the center of us all, where they led the stretches. At that point, I was already learning new things that would affect me for the rest of my life. The stretches involved much careful and precise movement. Nowadays, if I'm walking along and see some guy stretching, I can tell if he's a runner or not just by the way he stretches.

"Now we're going to do some form running, this is a warm-up we will do before every practice and every race. It will loosen up your body and help with running form. Now if you'll get in rows, then the first person in each row will make their way down about 25 meters while running in a specific form, and they will come back to the end of the line in a different form. I will tell you what forms to do. If you have never done this before, then stand in the back of the lines, and watch the upperclassmen.

I followed other freshman to the back of the lines. We all stood in a small field next to the trail. The heat of summer was intense, but the first faint breezes of fall were helpful. I noticed a stream of sarcastic confidence across the faces of most of the lean-looking upperclassmen in the front of the lines. They knew that they were being looked up to. They knew that we had no idea what to do, and they knew that we knew that they knew what they were doing.

"High knees!" Coach shouted. The front row of young men and women broke out from their lines while swiftly lifting their knees to their chests with each leaping stride. They stopped about 25 meters ahead of us all. The second group had already started for the other end, lifting their knees as high as they could. *So this is form running...* Eventually, all the rows high-kneed themselves to the other end and it was our turn. I quickly lunged my right knee up as high as I could while taking a small leap forward. By the time my group got to the end, the first group had already started to make their way back to the other end with a different form. "Fast high-knee!" Coach shouted. Under heavy breaths, I watched the upperclassmen do the same thing with their knees on the way back, but the knee pump was twice as fast. My leg muscles began to burn, but the burning felt good. It told me that I was already working them and making them stronger.

"Butt kicks!" He shouted. We ran to the other end while kicking our butts with our feet. Then we did skips, bounds, and all sorts of awkward, comical dances to the other end. The exercises looked so ridiculous while the stern faces of the runners concentrated on their forms. We spent about as much time form running as we did stretching.

Then it was time to run. Coach divided us up into groups: an advanced group who was running six miles, a middle group who was doing four, and a beginner group who was doing two. I, with not the highest confidence in my physical ability but with better self-esteem than to run with the slow group, ran with the middle group. I convinced Gilleland to come with me.

We ran the peaceful trail around campus. It went up and down hills through a thicket of shady woods. It was like the trees were blocking all of the noise and keeping peace inside the woods. I became winded pretty soon after we started, but it was nothing I couldn't handle. I remembered running track back in elementary school. My dad would tell me to breath in my nose and out my mouth to better control airflow in my body. I ran ahead of all the girls, and alongside this guy named Justin. Justin was a freshman also. He hadn't gone to Bode. He came from a different middle school in St. Joseph. He was about my same height with dark brown hair and random freckles. He was nice, and we instantly bonded because it was easy for us to run at the same pace and talk to each other, though he did most of the talking. When I run, I usually don't have much extra breath to talk, but I was a good listener. If anything, Justin came off as a little dorky to me because he wouldn't stop talking about cars and girls. I liked him though. We finished the four miles together.

91

When finishing a distance run with someone else, even after just one, you gain a unique bond and sense of companionship. What coach said to us earlier started to become apparent to me after I finished with Justin. "We run together. We sweat together, laugh together, and cry together." During my run, I noticed how close the upperclassmen were, with all of their little inside jokes. They seemed to understand and love each other like brothers. Cross-country was more of a camaraderie than a sport, and I liked it.

• • •

August, 1999

413 kids in my freshman class tumbled through the hallways of Central High School for the first time. There, on that day, it began. Everyone took the first step into becoming what they are. The men and women peeked out of their child bodies for the first time. Immediately upon busting through the doorways, I was overtaken by roaring masses of curious students filling the enormous halls all around me. I recognized a bunch of faces from middle school, and I laid eyes on hundreds of strangers.

This… is high school… Everything about it was so big. All my life I'd been little. All my life I had looked up to my big sisters in high school, all of their cool friends, all of the cool things they got to do. I remember the guys who were trying to get to my sisters were always sucking up to me and calling me "dude" with little personalized handshakes. They were so cool. So if I liked them, then they had the advantage with my sisters. They were all so cool. *Now it's my turn…*

The walls of our first-hour English class were covered with quotes about respect and posters of women with their fists in the air. As we walked in, Aretha Franklin's "Respect" was blaring on the speakers. Our body-builder of a teacher first told us about the importance of respect in high school and then she asked us to stand, introduce ourselves and say what we did at Central.

Jerry Field was the name of the first guy that stood up, and as he started to speak I could tell he was one of those slightly socially-out-of-sync folks. You know… people who say weird things out loud and giggle before anyone can tell if an actual joke was told. Jerry's hair was short, dark, a little shaggy and uncombed. There were a few oil spots on his black shirt, and his jeans fell a little short of covering his black shoes. He wore glasses that gave him a stereotypical nerd appearance. He said that he likes cars and motorcycles, the army, and "you know, guy things." He then giggled. Nobody else giggled, but I noticed that Jerry had briefly glanced at me during his giggle. It was an expectant glance, as if I were holding out on him when no one else was giggling. It's like he saw in me a considerate relation to his dorkiness. Perhaps we were connected. *I do have an almost bald head… and giant ears…* After a few more people, I stood to tell about myself. "I'm Johnny Cathcart Everyone! I'm on the cross-country team, and…"

After class, I purposely took some extra time to gather my books into my bag so I could walk out next to Jerry, who cautiously let others out before him. I walked up next to him as he exited into the hall. For a couple seconds, we just walked side-by-side. I pretended to suddenly notice him, and I made some comment about the teacher, intentionally drawing a small laugh and breaking any layers of ice that may have loomed between us. "So… power for women huh?" He looked at me, studied my suspicious intention for talking to him, finally realized that it was just to be friendly, and smiled.

"I think it's an excuse for not getting any," he replied.

Surprised by his sudden perverse comment on our 50 year old teacher, I gave him an awkward look and we both chuckled. "I'm Jerry," he said as he held out his hand.

"I'm Johnny, nice to meet you dude." I shook the hand; I was surprised by how firm his grip was for such a small guy.

Jerry found his place in high school with the JROTC, a program for those who are interested in the armed forces. All of the JROTC people kind of shared the same concerned, reality-based, literal attitude toward others in the world. Jerry had friends there who shared his sense of humor and understood him, and since he became friends with me, he introduced me to many of the JROTC people. Jerry knew about what happened to me in the seventh grade, so he would tell them. They were all interested and would ask me about it. Eventually, several of the army guys from school became my friends. Although it was gone, they all thought of my cancer as some perilous killer that would get to me again unless they did everything they could to overwhelm me with friendliness and comfort. They felt the need to protect me – to destroy my past enemies as if they still lingered in the hallways.

7
Practice After School

September, 1999

The locker room was a small, rectangular room with a few rows of rusty lockers and some benches. The tan paint peeled all around the brick walls and ceiling, and the toilet in the corner was barely enclosed by some ripped up stall doors. The room was filled with about 15 or 20 male cross-country athletes stripping off their clothes and loudly cracking lewd inside jokes. Entering athletes would run up to whip an undressing athlete in the butt with a towel, and everyone would laugh hysterically at the red marks we left on each other. Other guys would wrestle. Meanwhile, there would be loud races for the first to get in the toilet to let everything loose before practice. Most of the time, I was one of the last to make it there. Either that, or I was skipped in line because the upperclassmen always had "first poops." Freshman always got the worst end of the deal.

There was hooting and howling about the rank smells in the toilet. Along with the joy of the loud and crude atmosphere in the locker room, the toilet was one of the most treasured places of the Central cross-country team. While sitting at the toilet, one could read generations of inside rumors and jokes all over the walls, some marks were from the early 90s or before. The pen and marker on the inside walls of the toilet would fade over the years, and new jokes were always scribbled in by new cross-country athletes. The stall was special because it was more or less our team's stall.

After being pushed farthest back in line and being the last to hold my breath at the toilet that afternoon, I found myself a seat on the old wooden benches to change into my running clothes. I slipped off my nice shorts and street shoes and put on my sleeveless shirt and running shoes. While changing, I noticed in the mirror how my body was already changing due to a month of cross-country running. My legs appeared more lean and defined than before, and

95

with a healthier complexion. My stomach had tightened around swells of muscle.

I wasn't finding my shorts in my bag. Every once in a while somebody would steal a person's shorts and throw them outside the door so the pant-less owner would have to appear in the hallway to get them. I didn't see them in the hall, so I assumed I must have forgotten them. *I can't go to practice in my school shorts or in my underwear…*

It was getting late and most guys had already changed and left the locker room, but there were a few left. I asked my friend Peter if I could borrow some. He began taking his own off, I stopped him. Then I turned around to the last guy left in the room, my friend Johnny Rivera, a varsity runner. He had already pulled a spare pair of shorts out of his bag for me to wear. I looked at them for a minute and decided that I might just as well go in my underwear. The shorts were just shy of four inches long, and they were a shiny hot pink. On the sides were little slits that went up the leg even further. "Gee thanks man…" I said to Johnny as he grinned cynically. We left the school, hopped in his old rusty pickup and made our way across St. Joe to the College.

The rest of the team was already stretching next to the trail by the time we pulled up. Since we were late, we already drew suspicious looks from most of the team, including Tom O'Brien. I stepped from the car, and noticed more and more faces squinting in my direction as I started approaching them. I smiled proudly as if nothing was wrong. As Johnny Rivera and I walked closer, everyone was clearly looking at my shorts. There were a few whistles and hollers, but I acted normal and joined them in stretching. Tom O'Brien rolled his eyes, as if he had expected nonsense like this from his athletes.

On that day, Coach had us play the "rainbow game." He set eight cones out around the college campus; each with a different color marker under it. Our task was to take a card, run the long distance between each cone, and mark a color on the card. Each of us runners would mark all of the colors in a different order. When we got done, we tried to match our order of the colors with

Coach's. The one that matched Coach's order would win an extra popsicle at the end of practice.

I was totally winded and beaten by the last leg of the run towards the last color marker. That's when I heard a flirty voice call out from behind me, "Those are some hot pants Johnny!" I slowed my jog for a second to look around. I didn't see anyone, but the voice was a girl. I struggled to regain the energy I wasted by looking. I slowed to a lagging walk as I caught up with Justin and we joined the group of out-of-breath athletes at the bottom of the hill. Coach was standing there with a box of popsicles and a card.

• • •

Our first meet was that Friday at Swope Park in Kansas City. Several of the meets were scheduled for weekdays, and that always meant we'd only have about two hours of school.
The Central Cross-Country team has many traditions. One of them is called a CCCC (Concealed Cross-Country Comrade). It was a secret-Santa type thing. On the morning before each meet, every member of the team would bring gifts for his or her CCCC. They would usually fill some bag with a bottle of Gatorade, a couple of energy bars, and a gag gift of some kind, then wrap it up in something fun or ridiculous and leave the bag in Coach's room with the concealed person's name on it. Each runner would find his or her gift in Coach's room before we all left for the meets.

Everyone was gathering in Coach's room to get ready and leave for the Swope Park meet. I entered the room to join a group of finely-tuned athletes all fully clad in intimidating blue Central Cross-Country uniforms. Everyone was checking out the gift from their CCCC. I looked around for mine, and noticed a brown sack sitting on a desk in the middle of the crowded room.

There was a name on it, and I stared for a good several seconds as the conversations around me faded away into the distance for a second. The energy of the name seemed to call out to me. "It's got a ring to it," a girl said to me from behind. A smile grew on my

97

face, and I gathered my bags, my Gatorade, Powerbars, and my new cross-country name; Johnny Hotpants.

8
Truman Invitational

September, 1999

It was a great feeling to walk out of school while everyone else was still stuck in their hot, boring classes. I was dressed proudly in my Central Cross-Country uniform along with about 60 other teammates of freshman, junior varsity, and varsity guys and girls. There were two rumbling buses waiting for us on the street; one for the girls and one for the guys. On the side they read, "St. Joe Central." Coach stood by the guys' bus with a clipboard as he checked off names.

I've never been on a school bus when I wasn't being taken to or from school. *This bus ride has a real purpose. I am getting on this bus because I am an athlete, and I'm on a mission to compete.* We were like an army troop being shipped off to a battle. Each of us had our own special personalities and talents, and I was Johnny Hotpants. The fact that I had a nickname made me feel like an important member of the squad.

I elbowed my way through the crowded aisle in the bus. There were so many other guys shouting and wrestling for good window seats in the back while ripping open bags of chips and Powerbars.

All the upperclassmen sat in the back yelling "Freshman double up!" There were way too many guys on the bus for everyone to have their own seat, so several had to sit with someone else. Considering the long trip we had ahead of us, a seat all to yourself, where you were free to stretch, sleep, and lay out all of your stuff, was a luxury that freshman or sophomores didn't have. After being lectured about doubling up, I found a seat by Justin in the middle of the bus. He had his two bags, one of books and one of running things, and I still had mine to fit in. I had a pair of extra shoes, a pillow, and the little bag from my CCCC. I poked my head in the aisle to see what others were doing. The upperclassmen were pulling all sorts of food out of their bags. They had CD Walkmans, packages of grapes, hand-held video games, pillows, blankets, or books to read. I found a way to situate my legs over our bags with one leg out in the aisle and the other over the seat in front of us, rested my head on my shoulder, and closed my eyes.

The bus pulled up to a gigantic parking lot filled with hundreds of cars. There were about 20 school buses. Cross-country teams from around Northwest Missouri were piling out of them with their own flashy colors: green, yellow, blue, purple, gold, and orange. I began sizing people up. Most of the guys were tall and skinny with dark hair. They looked a lot older than me.

It suddenly seemed like everyone was in a hurry. The intensity of the moment must have been flowing through the ground like electricity because the second I stepped down on it, I became awake and alert as the music pumped in my ears. *Eye of the Tiger* by Survivor was blasting through the air from a set of loud speakers standing on a hill behind some trees. The hill was about 100 meters away from us. Next to the speakers was a big yellow tent. On the top of the tent there was a big banner that shouted in bold letters, "WELCOME TO THE 1999 TRUMAN INVITATIONAL."

This was the first and the biggest meet of the year. Hundreds and hundreds of people scrambled all around, helping to set up tents for their team, getting ready to race, or coming to watch their family in action. There were about 30 different big tents all around the hill, each of them a different color that had the team name slapped across the roof. There were more teams arriving and carrying up their tents. Beyond the massive accumulation of people and tents was a gigantic field. At the end of the field there stood an enormous stone castle overlooking the park. Ascending from the roof was a humongous cross. The top of it stood nearly 100 feet in the air.

Coach opened up some storage compartments under the bus. The upperclassmen grabbed the kit for the tent. We freshman grabbed the water jugs.

Once we found a spot amongst the chaos, we threw stuff down and the upperclassmen started putting together the tent. The tent came in a small package, but it expanded to about 10 feet high and 8 feet wide. The roof was royal blue, our school color. On the top it read "Central Indians Cross-Country." I stood by Gilleland as I watched everyone put together the tent. Coach yelled, "The freshman girls race starts in 30 minutes, so everyone better start walking the course. If you're a freshman or if you don't know the course, then follow the upperclassmen." Coach sure seemed to like the upperclassmen. He referred to them a lot as if they were wise ones that were designated to lead the way.

Before each race, the runners all walked the course in order to get a feel for the hills, the turns, the straight-aways, and whatever other unexpectable terrain might be looming around the corners. A group of upperclassmen guys were already walking toward the course. Gilleland, Justin, and I followed.

The course was about an eight feet wide path through the grass that had been mowed over. The starting line was in the middle of the field and was about 100 meters wide. The first 300 meters looked like a long uphill struggle. Once the course passed our tent, the hill took a steep incline of about 30 meters. The hill went straight toward the big church. Once the hill flattened, about 100 meters back from the church, it took a sharp left turn and went straight for about 100 meters, only to take another sharp left turn down the hill. Then the path wound through some trees downhill and straightened out for a while until it hit the first mile mark. White paint stained the grass on this spot with a big "1 MILE." I stopped for a second and looked back over the field and the ground we had covered. It seemed like we'd been walking forever. I already had to rest my hands on my knees for a breath.

We continued for about 200 more meters and the course finally turned to the left around a tree. It went back farther away in the general direction of the parking lot. We could see from here that it eventually made a U-turn to come straight back towards the mass of tents and the starting line where it ended. We skipped over the U-turn to the finish line, and headed for our tent. The course we just walked, and one more half loop around, totaled 3.1 miles, a solid 5k cross-country race. As we jogged back, everyone's movements quickened as the electricity in the air was heating up.

The freshman girls were jogging over to the starting line in a tight pack. There were seven of them, each slender and toned with long hair tightly pulled back in braids. A couple of them wore shades that hid their pretty faces, blocking some sun, but more importantly equipping them with a look of daunting intimidation. They looked like a pack of hungry wolves. The music sent waves through the air. I looked out at about 30 or 40 ferocious packs of freshman girls gathering around the starting line. The music was now "We are the Champions" by Queen. The song wasn't to the champion part yet, it was still "WE WILL WE WILL ROCK YOU… DU, BAH, DU-DU BAH, DU…" Coach was already down at the starting line waiting for the girls. There was an assistant coach still with us at the tent. His name was Coach Roger Price. His personality was nothing like Coach O'Brien's. Coach Price was more down-to-earth with a Kermit the Frog sense of humor. His friendly personality helped shade his authoritative standing as assistant coach.

He was also very smart. In fact, he taught physics at Central High School, and he was also a strong leader at the church I grew up in. Coach Price was full of intelligent quotes and words of wisdom. "It's natural to be nervous; this is our first race. If you're nervous, then you know that everything is working right. Being nervous only excites you, and that's good for the race."

At that, I nervously stripped down the warm-up uniform to my blue and white jersey. "BANG!" My back jolted with a shudder. I looked toward the sound. A swarm of people at either end of the course erupted with roars and cheers as the freshman girls took off. It was an amazing sight. Nearly 200 girls in a crowded straight line exploded out towards us with incredible power. I stood in awe as the bulk of runners whizzed passed with a strong gust of air that seemed to shake our tent. *That's going to be me?*

The rest of the team around me was hopping up and down, shifting from foot to foot, anything that got blood pumping for the race. I noticed two of my freshman teammates, Morton and Nathan. They kept quiet most of the time, like they were always

102

in deep thought, especially Nathan. He was Coach Price's son, and deep thought was in his blood. Nathan and Morton were two of the better runners on the team. Both of their wise faces focused on something I could not see as they jumped from side to side. "In order to take off in the midst of your physical peak, you want your heart to be beating fast and sweat to be peeping out of your skin before you start a race," Coach Price had said.

I hadn't seen my family yet. They were supposed to meet me there. *I hope they got the right directions...* I needed to know they were there watching me. I remember as a child whenever I would discover new things I could do with my world I had to make sure my parents were watching. "Mom, Dad, look at me!"

I was still trying to shake my nervousness away when Coach Price announced, "Time to head down boys!" *OK, this is it...* I started jumping from foot to foot while punching at the air. I felt so strong and so ready. I felt this was the final way to stomp out my cancer for good. What I went through was terrible, and I was ready to take vengeance upon it. The idea of this gave me a great sense of glory, and I concentrated on that. *That stupid cancer... I trampled it in the face. Now nothing can stop me. I am stronger than ever!*

"Are you coming Johnny?" Gilleland asked. With a release of breath and no words, I jogged over to him and the rest of my team. I looked at the athletes I was standing next to, and how in sync we were with our thick legs and Central Indians jerseys. I started to think that was all the motivation I really needed, then I noticed Mom, Dad, and my two sisters running to find me before my race started. I jogged up to them. They gleamed with pride. "We're sorry we're so late honey." Mom said as she was catching her breath. "At first we couldn't find the place and it took a long time to park." Dad gave me a high five. "Go get 'em!" Mom shouted with embarrassing parent-like enthusiasm that no one could ever live without.

There were already some of our competing guy teams warming up at the starting line. They were doing form running. We arrived to the slot of the starting line we had been previously assigned. There were lines all along the starting line dividing it into slots, marking where each team was to stand. We all gathered together and continued jumping around. I could feel the heat of anticipation grow along the line as more and more teams gathered.

A roar of screaming and shouting erupted again as the freshman girls neared the finish line. There were so many of them. There was a thick pack of girls in the front, and two of them were about 20 meters ahead of the rest. I didn't get a good look at the faces, but I could see that one of the two front girls was wearing a Central uniform. I couldn't see the finish chute either, because a thick crowd blocked it on either side. Within the next five minutes, almost the entire group of girls passed through the finish chute. A lot of girls had stopped toward the end of the race and started walking. Those girls finished about a minute or two after the main mass of racers, and by that time the crowd had gone away.

Every freshman boys team was on the starting line when the last girl finished. There were about 20 teams of freshman guys and about 200 some runners. We were doing *our* form running, going out about 15 meters from the line and back. We also did practice starts where we practiced how we were going to position ourselves and then break out whenever the gun popped. "The first 300 meters," Coach O'Brien said, "are the most important of the entire race."

A gun popped. It was the five-minute gun, warning us that our race was about to start. The gun seemed to pop a little more nervousness into all of us. It would be everyone's first race. We did a final practice start. When the whole team stopped, we started to huddle up. I'm not sure what we were huddling up for, but it just seemed appropriate at the moment. One of my good friends Curtis Calloway stepped up as a natural leader. Everyone gathered in the huddle and Curtis said, "All right guys this is it. Let's pray."

Now I didn't think that cross-country was a Christian group; it wasn't really. Some people I knew on the team actually seemed the opposite of what most people think of as "Christian." However, it seemed the adrenalin in the moment caused everyone to bow their heads. I looked up and all eyes were already closed within our compact group. Curtis started, "Dear Lord, we thank you for this ability you have given us to come out here and run this race. We pray that you will be with us as we run, and keep us and our competitors free from injury. Help us to be strong together as a team, and to do our best Lord, Amen." I silently didn't participate in the group prayer though. I was certain that if we tried to get God involved, then He would just throw some sort of obstacle in our way, perhaps by making us trip and getting malignant bumps on our heads.

We broke our huddle and started to jog back to the starting line, where most of the other teams were breaking their huddles with some sort of group-effort shout like "Go Team!" or "Tigers!" We got into the positions we were going to take off in. The faster guys were up front with one foot on the starting line, a few others and myself were right behind them. Coach O'Brien was right behind us all, giving us a few last words of advice in his loud, monotone voice that was surprisingly motivating. "Get out quick you guys, and stay to one side. Don't get caught up in the funnel. Be strong now."

The 100 meter starting line was filled with 200 runners, each ready to push their body to its extreme limits within the next 3.1 miles. The center of the line was probably the worst place for a team to be, because when everyone breaks out, they all run toward the path marked out for the course, which is only about 3 or 4 meters wide, creating a huge funnel when the two sides cave on the runners in the middle. We were on the far left side, with only two teams to the left of us that could cut us off into the center.

The line was jam-packed with teams in position and ready to race. A large man with a cowboy hat waddled out in front of us, about 100 meters from the line. He had a gun, and I trembled at what he was about to do. He shouted so we all could hear, "Now I'm going to hold my arm straight out like this, and then raise my arm slowly. When it gets over the top of my head, I'll fire the gun. If runners start early, then you'll hear the gun again and well do a restart, if anyone trips within the first 100 meters, then we'll do a restart. I wish the best of luck to you all."

105

The beat of hearts pulsed heavy vibrations into the air. My muscles tensed as the man began to lift his arm. The time that goes by as the gun is lifted is the longest of any cross-country race. The shear anticipation that gushes through every runner's veins wipes the mind clear of any thought.

400 eyes set a fiery gaze upon every slight movement of the gun so closely that I wouldn't have been surprised if it suddenly burst into flames.

BANG!

The crack pierced through the air with such a raucous boom that for a split second after it was over, time almost stopped. The runners remained tense with their first leg lifted past the line and their back leg muscle straining to push forward the weight of the body. The screams of the crowd were nothing but wide-open jaws petrified by the moment's impact. Reality jolted back into play as our first steps of the race slammed to the earth. The crowd's roar pounded through the air, and an explosive gust of wind shook the whole atmosphere.

The world seemed to fast-forward to make up for the lost time. All of my strength blasted into my legs like a suddenly un-kinked water hose. Immediately, a giant mass of runners started to cave in. Everything I was thinking before had vanished. The only thing on my mind was getting out of the funnel without falling and being trampled. It was like being in the middle of a tornado. The blur of runners breaking in was so fast and spontaneous. I can compare the feeling to driving 70 miles per hour down the highway while bumper-to-bumper with hundreds of other cars. If one runner were to trip, then he would take 50 down with him, and get stomped on by a lot of spiked feet. Shoulders clashed as everyone elbowed through to get a good spot. Flakes of mud and grass shot up everywhere as running shoes ripped through the moist ground for traction. The funnel narrowed into a crowded line as we all moved forward. The crowd let loose as the pack flew past the tent area.

We were approaching the first hill and the narrow path. The length of the mass of runners was about two hundred feet now, and we were still way too wide to fit on the course. I was in the middle of the line. I thought my best bet was to wedge my way out to the side where I could run freely up to the front of the pack. I looked both ways, and I was completely trapped by bodies. I eyed a skinny path through some runners and jumped through them to get out to the side. I was significantly smaller than most of the people around me, so I could squeeze through them without much trouble. By that time, I was sprinting fast and using up a lot of energy. On the side, I sprinted past as many runners as I could before we all hit the marked course where we were stuck in our positions for a while. The first turn came quick, and I was on the inside of it. I noticed the stone church-like building on the right.

The second turn to go down the hill came on just as fast, and I was confident of my status in the race by then. I could see about 30 people in front of me, and that meant about 170 were behind. Justin was ahead of me by about 10 meters. I could see he was muscling his way up to the front. I didn't see anyone else from my team ahead of me. This scared me a little because there were other runners on the team that I knew were a lot better than me. *Then why weren't they up in the front of the pack? Especially Curtis, Morton, or Nathan?* The rapid fluctuation of air pumped pain through my lungs. We were headed down a long stretch which seemed to go on forever. The first mile marker appeared in the distance. It was like a mirage in the desert, I could feel it getting closer, but I never seemed to reach it. The long pack of runners had stretched and thinned now as everyone set their paces.

To my left I could see members of the crowd, especially parents, wind themselves by running to different parts of the course in order to see their team pass by, and whip out cameras for quick pictures. I saw Mom and Dad looking at me. Their smiles were so big; my dad's face was pumping with ecstatic excitement. Dad gave me a big thumbs up and shouted with an enthusiastic rasp in his voice "YEAHHHH JOHN!" Mom joined "GO JOHN! YEAH!" Their voices were quickly drowned out in the hundreds of other screams that flooded the course. My lungs pounded harder and harder. I looked back and noticed Morton coming up on me. Curtis was right behind him. I turned forward to see the 1-mile marker about ten meters ahead of me. Coach was standing to the left of the course by the mile mark. As I crossed, he yelled out "5:40!" *I'm doing awesome!*

My heavy breathing turned to a steady pant now. My leg muscles burned. Justin, now about 3 feet in front of me, glanced back. He didn't look as strong as he did before. His tongue was hanging out of his face like a thirsty dog. His run was wobbly. I could hear him grunt as numerous people started to pass him by.

About ten feet in front of me, someone in an orange jersey went down. Justin and I weren't the only ones starting to fall apart. It looked like the guy just tripped over his own feet. He hit the ground hard and rolled violently like he'd been thrown from a speeding car. There were about six runners right behind him that either had to jump to the side or actually leap over him. It happened really fast, and I sort of did both.

The long, giant worm of runners finally started to turn to the left and go down towards the parking lot. The front runners looked farther and farther away. I checked behind my shoulder after the turn. Morton and Curtis were closer to me. Justin still hobbled right beside me. I realized that I was getting passed as well. I wheezed and grunted like Justin. Curtis passed me on the left. He was strong in his form. He didn't look over when he gasped in between his sequence of breathy words, "C'mon Hotpants." In a split second he was gone, on his way to the front of the pack. Morton passed right behind him. "HOOOHH, HOOOHH..." Their breathing sounded strong and in control. "HUUUH, HUUUH..." My breathing sounded like I was giving birth. We passed the U-turn, and started back towards the hill. About four more runners passed me and faded into the growing pack up front.

We came up on the spot next to the tents, and there my parents were again. I could feel the sick, exhausted look on my face as I passed them by. They didn't seem to notice this, or the fact that I was about 20 runners back from where I was the last time they saw me. I could barely hear their screams, "GO JOHN! YEAH!" I was in my own little world, where everything on earth seemed blurs and mumbles. All I heard was the thunderous plunging of breath through my worn system that shook with every footstep.

All I could see was the dirt that flew in my face as runners passed me and roughed up the terrain ahead. All I could think of was how much I wanted for it to be over.

We had finished our loop and more than half the race. Now we were cutting back through the middle of the field. There was no sign of Justin now; he had fallen back far behind me. Nathan swiftly passed me to the left. He had no sign of struggle on his face, just concentration. Curtis and Morton were far ahead. Three more Central guys passed me, one-by-one.

Behind, the crowd was already racing to the finish chute to watch the first runners come in. I was turning to make it up my last hill. I remember Coach O'Brien saying, "The hill is the best place to pass people, because most of them are weak, and they lose it on the hill." I was weak. The hill hit me hard. My trudging up the hill slowed enough to be a fast walk, but in my mind I was still running. I was going as fast as I could go. Runners passed me right and left like I was nothing but a crippled pedestrian in the way. At that point, I no longer worried about how many runners passed me; I just wanted to finish. The pain was horrible. Wind battered through my chest like a trapped bee in a jar. My jelly legs burned everywhere. Finally I made it to the end of the hill and turned right for the final straightaway. Then, it was a last turn back down the hill, and a break for the finish chute. The giant church was now on my left; the presence of the giant cross weighing down on me from above. About 30 runners must have passed me on the hill, and it looked like about half had finished already. The thought was all too precious: the agony was about to end.

There was nothing left in me. The chute was about 200 meters away now. The turn to the finish lay just ahead, and perhaps because of wanting so badly for everything to be over with, my numb legs jolted with electricity and I started sprinting. I shaved the last corner, and I was now flying on my toes towards the finish. The chute glowed like the gates to Heaven in that play. I entered into what I like to call the mind-over-body experience. This is a state the body reaches in a cross-country race, usually during the final sprint, where the runner no longer controls his/her body. It happens when every limit of physical effort has been manually exceeded, and the body is empty of gas. Strength or endurance does not come into play during this state - only mind, will, and heart. Coach Price says that when you get to the end of what your body can do, that's where faith begins.

The pack had spread out so far now, that there were only about four other runners remotely close to me as I was running toward the finish. One was too far ahead for me to catch up, and three were behind me a good enough distance that it seemed they could not catch up. The crowd blared to my left and right as I let my body carry me into the long chute. My heart pumped at its full limit, and could not be driven any further. However, when I was about 15 feet away from the finishing line, some runner dashed from behind and passed me. It hurt to see someone pass me like that, like I was nothing.

I finally broke through the magical veil that suddenly shut everything off. My last leap over the line hit the ground, and my body immediately went limp and wildly flopped to an exhausted halt. It was like the whiplash end to a wooden roller coaster. After the line, the chute thinned out for about 15 more meters. This was the point where the meet officials handed out place numbers to all the finishers. There were about ten half-dead runners slowly being guided through the chute at the same time as me, thus clogging it and making other runners who had just crossed the line stop instantly like they ran into a brick wall.

This was where the world you were in during the race disappears and reality stumbles its way back into sight. Walking is hard right after a race. It's like after ice skating for a while; walking doesn't feel right.

Multiple arms from strangers grabbed at me to hold me up as I made my way through the chute; it was like trying to make my way through a tunnel of spider webs, or like Princess Ariel and the poor unfortunate souls. One lady shoved a card in my hand. I barely had enough juice left in me to read the number on the card: "151."

It looked like an F on a grade report. I glanced at it for maybe a fourth of a second, and a wave of cold self-pity ran down my spine. I knew I couldn't have done anything more. I ran my hardest the entire way, and my hardest - my own mind-over-body experience - just wasn't good enough.

I popped out of the chute, and stumbled around looking for nothing in particular to fall onto. Hundreds of beads of sweat rapidly appeared and ran down my face like condensation in one of those Coors Light commercials. My limp body was about to lose control. Mom was jogging up to me, her smile so big. "Ohhh honey!" I could tell she was gleefully proud… proud of my 151 placing. *At least I didn't get last.* I aimed toward Mom's arms and collapsed.

9
Check Up

May, 2000

The ringing in my ear buzzed louder and louder across Interstate 70 towards St. Louis. Once we hit the big Arch, we would turn south toward Memphis.

Two weeks prior, my freshman year had come to an end. Most of my hair had grown back, I was athletic again, and amazingly, I had been elected class president for the next year. I was well on my way to becoming a normal healthy teenager.

We were traveling across the country to my regular three-month checkup at St. Jude. The ten-hour trip would always suck energy from me. Mom minded her driving while I sat in the passenger seat trying to keep myself busy by fantasizing about being a hero of some sort - risking my life to rescue a girl from a psychotic turtle. Girls that I knew would be caught helpless somehow in the face of danger, I would usually save them with my martial arts skills. When I was really bored, I would ask Mom complicated questions like how things worked. It was tough to fall asleep. If I tried to sleep sprawled out along the back seat, then the hard seat belts would poke me in the back. The front seat wasn't a good place to sleep either, because I'm just not good at falling asleep while sitting up.

One thing I will always have vivid memory of is the powerful entrance to Memphis. Whenever entering the city through the gigantic suspension bridge over the Mississippi River, the skyline of old buildings on the other side overwhelms me. To the right of the bridge, a large sign greets everyone who crosses, *"Welcome to Memphis, Home of the Blues, Birthplace of Rock and Roll."* It is a special feeling when driving into Memphis, a place filled with so much history. It's a place with a long background of racial tension and revolution, a place of battle, deep roots, and a place with a real song to sing, mostly on the blues pentatonic scale.

Besides all of the excitement, I also get an uncomfortable shiver down my back. St. Jude Children's Research Hospital lies to the left of the bridge. The massive complex of light tan buildings stands off to the left of downtown on its own campus. The buildings are wide and tall, with a set of enormous bright red letters on the top of the fattest building, St. Jude Children's Research Hospital.

As the hospital seemed to hold my eyes tight, painful memories began to flash through my head: images of hairless children fighting for their lives and looking so helpless at the mercy of big machines. The sounds of painful screams and whiny babies filled my ears. The smell of the radiation filled my head like Pavlov's dog slobbering at the ring of the bell.

The entrance to the hospital is a large wrought-iron gate. There is a man in a station by the gate that greets everyone who comes in and opens up the gate for regular patients. He sits in a small booth like a toll collector all day long, watching over the entrance to St. Jude's. This is always an older, jolly man who could just as well be a train stationmaster, waving happily to each and every train that passes. Every time we passed through the gate, the stationmaster found my eyes inside our vehicle and issued a very distinct wink. I think he did this for every patient because I could see him do it for cars in front of us whenever there was a line. Though nobody ever heard the stationmasters say anything but, "Alrighty, you have a nice day now!" he maintained a special unspoken relationship with each of the patients.

We pulled up to the gate and stopped. We used to have a card that indicated we were regular patients. But since we left in 1998, we have been strangers to the new stationmasters, and they ask us who we are every time. The friendly-faced black man in a security outfit walked out to us from his little station. He saw me and could tell that I was an old patient.

"How ya doin' today ma'am?" he said to Mom with a deep jazzy voice.

Mom replied, "We have John Cathcart, coming for a checkup."

"OK… and what's that numba?" "15090," she answered. 15090 is my patient number. I believe I am the fifteen thousand and ninetieth patient. I go back nowadays and patient numbers are in the high 40,000s.

"Alrighty… have a nice day now!" He winked at me again as the gate slowly opened and we drove into a large circular drive in front of the hospital. The expansive yard was still as beautiful as it always had been: bright green, nicely cut and edged along the clean sidewalk that leads into the main entrance. Memphis has thick, springy grass. The drive curves around under the heavy awning enclosing the main doors, similar to the entrance of a fancy hotel. Between the large columns of tannish pink stucco stands an Olympus sized statue of St. Jude Thaddeus in a robe, honorably praying with a Bible in his hand.

According to the Gospel, St. Jude was a brother of St. James. In Matthew 13:55, he is described as the "brethren" of Jesus, probably his cousin. He is traditionally depicted carrying the image of Jesus in his hand. This represents the imprint of the divine Countenance that was entrusted to him by Jesus. He is the patron saint of seemingly impossible or difficult causes. St. Jude is known to be a true friend and a beacon of hope to those in need who call on him.

Across the drive, opposite the entrance, is a beautiful pavilion with a golden dome at the top. It is called the Danny Thomas Pavilion, a monument and grave for the founder of the hospital and famous sitcom star Danny Thomas. As the story goes, when Danny Thomas was a young and unknown actor, he prayed to God that if He would help him become successful in his career, then he would build God a shrine… St. Jude's.

A little bit before the entrance, the drive splits in two. One path takes you around the rest of the hospital campus, and one goes up in front of the main doors. We took the path around to a small parking lot that surprisingly had a few open spots. "Hooray! We're here!" Mom exclaimed to me happily, attempting to lighten up the situation.

As we approached the main entrance, more and more memories stirred in my head: memories of nurses and doctors I had made friends with, memories of certain whiny kids I dreaded seeing every day, memories of loud intercoms constantly blaring through the hallways, "JOHN CATHCART, JOHN CATHCART, PLEASE COME TO WHATEVER – CLINIC!"

The legendary stone eyes of St. Jude Thaddeus seemed to follow me as I passed under him.

Mom held my hand as if she were walking me across the street as a boy. We came through large glass revolving doors to the front lobby. To either side of us was a row of comfy sitting chairs. These are not really waiting rooms, but more like sunrooms. The sun shines through the big windows all around the front lobby, and people sit in the chairs and think, read, or wait for whatever is worth waiting for. Upon entrance to the hospital, we saw children everywhere. Some were being wheeled around in chairs, a few hobbled around on crutches, the really small ones were pulled around in wagons disguised as fire trucks or race cars.

None of the children had hair, but just a few lonely strands that survived the genocide of their curly companions and helplessly looked for a way to die peacefully and end the suffering. My hair knew how that was. The kid's innocent faces had all been washed with the same unhealthy, desaturated hues that cancer treatment brings.

Above us loomed a balcony from the second floor. From the balcony hung a large banner: "Welcome to St. Jude!" Actually, the front lobby *is* spectacular. There are big colorful pictures of children, celebrities involved with the hospital, artwork, and comfortable furniture all around. The entrance really makes a person feel like they are going to a big event.

On a normal checkup, we start off by registering at the front desk to get my appointment schedule and hospital wristband. We would do this every day back in 1997. Behind the desk, usually sat a large woman with glossy, well-sculpted hair and big blingy jewelry. Every lady had a big-lipped smile stretching from ear to ear.

115

Most people in Memphis have a specific Memphanian accent. They talk slow and deep, with a lot of bass, and a lot of men have a rasp. The large black ladies talk with a real sweet-Memphanian accent that always makes people smile, they're like grandmas with fresh cookies. "Heeey honey, what can I do yah for?" She asked me when I came up to her desk. Mom answered for me, "We're just here for a checkup, and we need to get a hotel for tonight." St. Jude's helps arrange and always pays for any housing or lodging for patients, whether a patient has to come everyday, or just come one or two nights a year for a checkup. They have deals with certain hotels in the area. We just have to let someone from the hospital know we're there, and they'll give us a ticket for a hotel room.

The lady replied, "OK now, what's that numba?"

"15090," I announced.

"Alrighty," she said. I looked up at Mom who, at only 5' 3" was still a tad bit taller than me. The chemo stunted my growth drastically. She looked at me and smiled with a scrunched nose and a squint. This is a special little smile she gives me sometimes when something is said that we can both relate to. I guess it was just a little ironic for Mom and I when we were asked to recite my patient number just as we did everyday three years ago. My patient number has become so metaphorical to Mom and I. It represents my whole cancer experience, and the adventures Mom and I have been through together. "OK," the lady at the desk said in a slow Memphanian style. "Here you go." She handed us a sheet with the appointment times for the next day and a ticket for a hotel. "You'll be staying at the Marriott, is that alright?" "That's great," Mom answered. St. Jude's offered us a shuttle bus to the hotel, but we took our car. The Marriott was just down the street.

• • •

Our wake-up call rang loud at 6:30 in the morning. Our first appointment, Assessment/Triage, was scheduled for 8:00 AM. Assessment/Triage has always been the default station we had to go to before we could go anywhere else in the hospital.

The hospital wristbands were a different color for every day of the week, and that day it was red. We went over to a small room behind the registration desk for Assessment/Triage, and sat in some blue chairs to wait.

Different nurse voices shouted out names from the intercom every so often. Most were loud - some so loud I would have to hold my ears. "LAWRENCE BADEN, LAWRENCE BADEN PLEASE COME TO AUDIOLOGY." "JORGE OLIVER, JORGE OLIVER, PLEASE COME TO A-CLINIC..." For every call, there was an emphasis on the first syllable of the first time they called a last name, and a lower, flatter tone the second time, almost like an auctioneer, "Thirteen, do I hear thirteen?" After ten minutes of noise from the overhead, "JOHN CATHCART, JOHN CATHCART, PLEASE COME TO ASSESSMENT/ TRIAGE!"

A nurse greeted me as she passed us in the hallway.
 "Well hi John, how are you?"

"Great, good to see you," I replied. "Right this way," she said. She led me to a little side exam room.

"Now just wait here John, and the nurse will be with you in a minute." *Surprising how they all remember my name... They seem to repeat it a lot... I guess so they won't forget.*

A hefty African-American lady came in, and I didn't recognize her. She strapped a blood pressure band around my upper arm while popping a thermometer in my mouth. The strap around my arm squeezed tight, and it was a bit uncomfortable when I could feel my blood straining under the pressure to budge its way through the arteries. Then she brought me to a scale that was built into the floor, and it read 52.1 kg. That meant I weighed about 116 lbs. "And how old are you now John?" she asked me. "Fifteen." Then she stood me straight up against a wall and recorded my height, which was about 5' 2".

117

I've been through this same routine about one hundred times, so I was sure I was done, but she then said, "You have some lab work ordered for today so I'm gonna have to take your blood."

I had gotten used to it, and had learned how to tolerate having my blood sucked, but I still didn't like it. Back in 1997 they didn't take blood at assessment/triage. "The Lab" was the place to go to get blood work done. For in-patients, their blood was checked everyday for a report of certain levels, such as platelets, and various blood cell counts. To be sent to "The Lab," used to be like a sentence to the principal's office. I was glad I didn't have to go there.

I watched closely as the nurse started to take things out of her drawers to use for my blood work: a couple of gauzes, some sterile wipes, towels, a giant rubber band to cut off my circulation, and... the butterfly needle.

She looked around on my arm for some of the juiciest veins visible. Similar to a babbling brook covered by snow and ice, she could see the active veins below my skin. She picked one, cleaned the area three times, tightly wrapped the band around my upper arm, and slowly brought the needle in for the kill. The needle and its tube resembled a snake slithering its way to my skin. The snake held my eyes as it plunged through. I could not only feel the sick insertion of foreign steel under the membrane of my skin, or the interrupted flow of blood being yanked back from my body into the needle, but I could see it. It was like the cereal Cinnamon Toast Crunch... "The taste you can see!"

Once she pulled the butterfly from my skin, she stuck it inside of this small test tube that acted as a vacuum and sucked the blood inside, where it could be sent to the back for testing.

An MRI was scheduled for me immediately after assessment/triage. We traveled down some familiar hallways to the MRI area, where we signed in at another desk and waited. The MRI waiting area is the same for radiation therapy - filled by blue couch/chairs. Just as all waiting room chairs, the cushions were colored with stains of pieces of emotion from the long history of sitters. The metal frames of the couch/chairs were the same bright red as the letters outside the building.

It was all routine for my mom and I, the checkup. We did Assessment/Triage, then MRI, and then we waited to be called in to the D-section where we meet with Dr. Gajjar. We would spend a minute catching up with him. Then he would tell us that the MRI scans look fine and free of any cancer remains, and finally Mom and I were free to make the long trip back home.

We had to go to the old triangle waiting room, which looked mostly the same as it was the first time I saw it. It was quieter though. Behind some chairs, at the peak of the triangle, were three computer stations where kids can play games while waiting. *These weren't here back in 1997… They have done some work on this place.*

We had already signed in at the D-Clinic, and were waiting for Dr. Gajjar to meet with us as usual. Mom and I were playing a nice healthy game of Battleship. After a few minutes, I was already winning. I had her battleship and her carrier sunk, and she had only destroyed my submarine.

Out of the blue, Dr. Gajjar appeared in our peripheral vision. I always enjoyed hearing Gajjar's voice; it sounds Arabic, with the rapidness of Spanish, and a hint of the congested voice of Billie Joe Armstrong, the lead singer of Green Day.

Gajjar proudly wears his dark skin with a scrunched, cheerful face and glasses that don't seem to serve any optical purpose, but only contribute to his unique character and aura of quick intelligence. I don't think I've ever seen him wear anything other than slacks with a well- starched, lightly-striped dress shirt and tie. His black, nicely-combed short hair has been the same since I first met him in 1997.

He walked right up to us without considering at all that he might have been interrupting our Battleship game. He greeted us as usual, then looked at us for a couple seconds in silence, as if he were thinking about what to say next. This wasn't normal because Gajjar usually speaks fast with no hesitation. He finally asked my mom if she could come back and talk with him for a moment… "alone." He assured me it would be about five minutes at the most. I nodded a confident nod as he walked away with Mom, gently patting at her back. I then looked back at my desolate and vulnerable ships, watching carefully as they silently floated in their positions, anxious for battle.

Ten minutes later, Mom slowly emerged from the shadows of the D-Clinic. "Hey, are we ready to go back?" I asked her. I didn't notice her face.

"Yeah…" she said. She performed an awkward pause then… "Let's play some more Battleship," she said. She seated herself on the blue cushion on the other side of the seat. Mom is a proper person. She always sits with good posture, but when she has overly excellent posture and a straighter than normal face, anyone in my family would know that there was something wrong - and that she was hiding from the moment with her hands daintily rested upon her lap. I looked up, noticed her position, and quickly glanced back at my boats, fearing they were about to be sunk by something more than opposing battleships.

10

Results

It was malignant. A Medulloblastoma tumor rarely grows back in the exact same spot on any patient. If there is ever a re-growth, then it usually ends up down bloodstream in some other part of the body, down the spine, or elsewhere in the head.

Dr. Gajjar had spent some time carefully reviewing the MRI scans, and spotted a bubbling mass of red jelly occupying the exact same portion of my posterior fossa, steaming hate, fueled by vengeance. The tumor had regained control of the exact same spot it once occupied at the base of my brain about 2 inches behind my right ear. These tumors rarely grow back after two years, especially after being "debulked" like a well-carved pumpkin, fried by six weeks of radiation, and poisoned by four rounds of chemotherapy. Survival rates of these tumors are a little better than 50/50. Survival of a re-growth of a Medulloblastoma tumor... is not enough to speak of. When they grow back, they come faster, stronger, and ruthlessly evil.

I don't remember how long the tears ran down Mom's face - whether for fear of returning to the front lines of battle, or losing her son to a battle that she thought had been won. Neither do I recall how long it took me to swallow the reality of the situation, just like the first time I heard of my cancer just a few years ago. We hid ourselves in each other's shoulders and cried. There must have been people around the waiting room looking - even people who didn't speak English – who knew by watching us, by relating to us on a level so deep among St. Jude patients... what news we had just received. My battleship, which I had so proudly defended, was now sinking under my own tears.

As I glanced around at the people in the room, memories started rushing into my head as if I were falling backwards in time. It was then that I started to drift off into a sort of intense déjà vu.

February, 1998 – St. Jude's Hospital

Imagine children's cough syrup - the sensation you get the second the disgusting red goo hits your tongue and you want to gag... Involuntarily, your mouth refuses to let it sit for more than a split second and quickly flushes it down your throat like a toilet. As it travels, it leaves traces of the thick red taste on the walls of your throat. Your eyes clamp shut and your head is thrown back as you cringe under the nauseating aftertaste that lasts for minutes. This is a good example of what chemo felt like, only multiplied several times. With chemo, the cough syrup is never swallowed, and it never settles in your stomach. It clings to not just your throat, but all over your body, poisoning every limb, gushing through every vein, shutting down your system in all regions, and brutally murdering any cell that even thinks about duplicating. In the heart of its rage, I had lost all of my strength, all of my color, and most all of my will to go on.

There I was lying on my bed in our apartment in Memphis, *"Home of the Blues," "Birthplace of Rock and Roll,"* reflecting on my first round of chemo - my first encounter with the beast - wondering how in the world I was supposed to go through three more of them. Just waiting to be infused with the destructive poison again within the next two weeks... I had nothing else to hope for, nothing else going for me. The only thing on my mind, was not the rational world of everyday "normal" worries, such as, "What am I going to wear to school today," or "I wonder where my girlfriend is," but an entire spectrum of awareness that all I could do was lie down flat, stare at the ceiling, and just take it... not minute by minute, not step by step, but as one everlasting presence of the hospital room. It was like I wasn't completely with my physical body. I could only view it from a third person's pessimistic point of view.

• • •

I felt sick. It had been a week and a half since my first round of chemo. My counts were down. Counts refer to levels of various blood cells flowing through the blood at a certain time. Every time they took blood, they checked my counts. We all have a WBC count, which is the number of white blood cells in the blood. This is the immune system component of blood that does most of the infection fighting. WBCs come in all different flavors, including segs (slang for neutrophils), eosinophils, basophils, and bands. These are usually expressed in percentages. Typically, there are 80% segs, 15% neutrophils, 4% eosinophils and 1% bands within normal blood. Each of these is critical to a healthy WBC count. A normal WBC is 5-10,000. If much lower than 5,000, then there is a risk of getting an infection because there are not enough WBCs to fight it off, even little everyday ones. During chemo, my WBC count spent most of its time around zero. It was like having temporary AIDS.

Deep within the stream of blood they suck up to examine, they also look carefully for red blood cells (RBCs). The RBCs flowing through your body are reflective of the amount of energy you have. Your RBCs carry oxygen from your lungs to vital organs such as your kidneys, brain, heart, muscles, etc… They also carry carbon dioxide away from those same organs, which is produced as a by-product of metabolism. Red counts are most often described in terms of hemoglobin (Hb) and hematocrit (Hct). Ultimately, they both measure the amount of blood in the body. Hemoglobin is measured by how dense the color of red is through a machine that measures light passing through the stolen blood sample. The measurement is expressed in grams of hemoglobin per deciliter, where essentially the color reading is transferred to the weight of blood determined through some impossible formula.

Normal hemoglobin is 12-14 g/dl. Hematocrit, on the other hand, is a percent of actual blood cells in a sample of blood. Blood contains RBCs and a fluid called plasma. To calculate your hematocrit they take a blood sample and put it in a small glass tube and spin it down in a centrifuge. The RBCs separate from the plasma and the doctors can then calculate the percent of RBCs to total volume simply by measuring with a ruler the length of RBCs in the tube and dividing it by the total length of fluid (RBCs and plasma) in the tube. A normal hematocrit is about 35 - 40%. During chemo, my red count hung extremely low. Little oxygen found its way to my vital organs and I was tired and empty. I would need a blood transfusion to survive and be rejuvenated. That is… a bag of someone else's saucy red blood, full of fresh WBC's and RBC's! Donated blood saved my life many times. (Go give blood or plasma)

···

Typical chemo day: By around four in the morning, most of the time I would realize that I wasn't going to get to sleep, and I would give up. First of all, I was too hungry to sleep. It wasn't just like a simple empty stomach, but more of an empty unhealthy feeling. Everything I'd try to eat, I'd throw right up. In fact, no food would even make the full trip down my esophagus to my stomach because, like a thermal circuit breaker, my stomach would recognize that food or drink was trespassing so it would automatically sever the connection and send it back up through my mouth, returned mail, invalid address. The empty feeling would come from what my stomach did take in… in absence of food. If the stomach goes so long without food, and it no longer has body fat to metabolize, then the body starts to take its own muscle fibers to eat. No matter how hungry someone gets, the stomach is always taking something whether or not anything is coming down the throat.

Also, chemo gives you an extreme case of acid reflux. It was hard to lie for more than a minute without swallowing a full eight ounces of acidy saliva that seemed to pump into my mouth from glands I never knew existed. I was constantly sitting up to spit into the little spit and hurl bowl next my bed. Many times I would get tired of sitting up, or I couldn't sit up at all, so I would place the spit/hurl bowl on my pillow, lying and spitting as I pleased.

I never had food in my stomach, so, when feeling like I had to hurl, I would just fall into these states of radical dry heaves. My heaves sounded like an extremely old man or a heavy smoker trying to laugh at a comedy club. My stomach eruptions became such a regular routine, that I grew indifferent to it. Most of the time, it wasn't a gross thing at all… nothing would come out. It would be sort of scary to someone who saw it for the first time. Mom and Kristin, who saw it multiple times daily, became as indifferent about it as I was. Don't get me wrong, they would always say something to me to show me they cared, and felt horrible for me and all, but really there was nothing anyone could do to stop it from happening. So, the best way to approach the unfortunate incident was with a "not that big of a deal" attitude. However, indifferent or not, the sensation to hurl came on so frequently that trying to sleep was nearly impossible. The few times I would be asleep at four in the morning, I would hurl in my dreams and wake up.

In addition to an empty hunger, severe acid reflux, and compulsive hurling, I believe one of the main reasons I gave up trying to fall asleep by around four in the morning was predominantly emotional. During the long hours of the night when Mom or Kristin were sound asleep in the adjacent room, my IV pump ticked and tocked, and the glare of the moon's light would mock me through the crack left open by the curtains covering my small window. During these times, I could not shut out the thoughts about wanting to be somewhere else. I wanted to be with my friends. I wanted to be in school. I wanted to be in sports. I wanted to be normal. The word "normal" was so depressing for me to think about. I kept getting these images in my head about how not-normal I would be for the rest of my life.

Once I had stared at the ceiling long enough, I would give up. This was when I'd usually wake up at six in the morning and realize that I had fallen asleep for a little bit. I used to think that if I just kept on day dreaming, then I would eventually fall asleep. But really the key is to stop thinking altogether. It seems you only fall asleep once you've given up on trying.

When I wasn't waking up early to hurl, I was waking to Jennifer. Jennifer was the nurse that took care of me during night and morning hours. The nurses were on a tag-team schedule. There were about thirty rooms on my floor, 15 on one wing and fifteen on the other. In the middle of each set of rooms was a nurses' station. They had a big circular desk filled with computers and office stuff. It was their home base, a sort of battle station. Three or four different nurses would hang out there during the day shift. Each nurse handled certain rooms, attending to the needs of those particular patients. Once their shift was done in the evening, another group of nurses would take their place for the night shift. Jennifer worked the night shift. In the early morning at about 5:30 or 6, she always turned on a light right outside my room and stepped in quietly as if she believed the light hadn't woken me. Jennifer came in many times during the night, and sometimes she would show up in the day.

There were a series of bags that hung from my IV pole, all attached to my line. The contents of each slowly dripped into me all hours of the day. There were four different IV bags on my pole: two gold ones, a sepia-toned one, and a yellow one. I'd sometimes mistake that one for urine at first glance. The three chemo bags and a fourth of something else hung from the same pole only on the first day of each round. The bags for the rest of the days were various drugs to keep me alive while I recovered. The bags all alternated their dripping. There was one bag from a separate pole that was dripping at all times every day. It was plain saline solution that kept me hydrated throughout my stay at the hospital. Two bags below it were filled with pain medication. One was a liquid form of Tylenol that would drip only occasionally. The other was morphine, which was incredible. I controlled it with a button and could have it whenever I wanted. I'd squeeze the morphine pump when I wanted to float away, literally, because morphine gives people that ability. On morphine, my body became too heavy and saturated to hold me in, and I just felt myself drifting out of it.

Jennifer stopped in a lot. In the early mornings when the world was still quiet and dark, she would come in one last time before her shift was over to check the status of the bags. A computer monitored all of them. She would get on the computer, type some stuff, and then come and check on my vital signs. Jennifer also brought me breakfast, which I could never eat. However, I would spend the rest of the morning talking with Mom, taking little pecks at the food, hurling, and then reading through my daily pile of get-well cards.

"What are you going to do when you're done with this one John?" Jennifer would ask. She meant this one round of chemo.

"I'd really like to go home," I'd say. They didn't like me to go home in between chemo rounds. They wanted me to stay close to the hospital in the event something went wrong, like a limb randomly falling off or something.

On some days, a different nurse would walk in during the afternoon: a plump black woman who looked like those at the front registration desk, and she was happy like them too. All of the women at St. Jude's were a little hard to tell apart because they were all equally kind and happy. This plump woman came in every three days with a small baggie of three different Q-tips. They were oversized Q-tips, the length of a pencil and the width of an index finger, that is, the width of a normal index finger; this lady's index finger was twice the size of an average index finger. She would come in and joke with me for a minute. Then she took the Q-tips and wiped them in three different holes of my body. She would wipe the first Q-tip in my mouth. She wiped the next one pretty far up my nostril (sometimes so far I could swear it touched the bottom of my eyeballs, and I would bleed), and then I would open the back of my gown to expose a good part of me so that she could wipe the third Q-tip where she needed to (never so far in as to cause a commotion). She took these samples and sent them to the lab. I'm not exactly sure why, but I know it was to test certain fluids and extracts from my body for things they needed to know.

All of the ladies, more so the well-fed ones, were very friendly people. As miserable as the chemo made me, I always kept my good sense of humor. One day the plump black lady came in ready to whip out her Q-tips. There were a pair of boxer shorts I owned that were nice and colorful and they had a rather accurate-looking rubber butt taking up the backside. (Some people thought those were my "Hotpants.") I knew that whenever the Q-tip lady came in, she would want to see part of my butt so that she could swab

127

at it. So one day, I wore my butt-shorts underneath my gown. She did my mouth and my nose. Then as she moved towards my butt, everyone in the room (me, Mom, and Dad) all hid our mischievous giggles under our breath like when you put salt in someone's drink while they're away from the table. She removed just enough gown to reveal what she thought was my bare butt, but it wasn't until she tried swabbing it that she realized it was fake. "Ha!" Dad exclaimed!

After two weeks of my daily routine as an in-patient, it was time for me to go home and rest. I would return for the second round two weeks after that. The day before I left, two nurses came into my hospital room with a frosty bag of grainy, yellowish liquid. It definitely wasn't the same red bag of another Good Samaritan's blood, which I got a lot of. Upon the bag's arrival, the entire room instantly filled with the nice cold aroma of dead fish with a nauseating sterile tinge added. There was condensation on the side because it was ice cold.

My half-open eyes turned over from being nestled deep in the pillow to watch as the nurse rolled in what looked like a six-foot clothes hanger with the yellow bag dangling from the top. "All right John, are you ready for a jump start? We are going to give you your bone marrow back!" Despite the uncontrollable enthusiasm building up in my mind, my sluggish nod of approval was enough to signal that I was in imperative need of it.

Gajjar had told me that I would feel the great effects of having fresh bone marrow in me almost instantly, and that it would not only give me the strength to sit up and open my eyes, but enough immunity power to walk out of the hospital. I would have to wear a light blue surgeon's mask to keep from getting infections. With the bone marrow back, my immune system would slightly exceed nonexistence, and any infections could be helped with emergency treatment. But it would still lack the strength to fight any more than a few infectious cells all by itself.

The nurse reached for the bundle of bandages on my chest in order to pump the bone marrow into my line. Though I was weak and tired, the second a foreign object dared cross into the vicinity of my line, I became extremely alert. She started taking off bandages to get to the little snake underneath. She hooked up a tube coming from the bag to my line, and opened up the stopper to let the liquid flow through towards my inside.

"Now, this is going to be very cold."

• • •

Back at St. Jude's, May, 2000

Mom and I cried our eyes dry, but we never let go of each other. Memories of Memphis faded into reality again and I eventually realized I had to face the present.

I guess I don't really get it… God. God… what are you anyway? Are you trying to tell me something? Is this like… your sick little way of getting your message across? What's your message this time?

I don't really think I was in prayer, so much as… boiling in my head at the first culprit I deemed responsible, the one with the cookie crumbles in his chin, more so the only one with the capabilities to do so. Who else to blame? I'm not sure if the anger inside was driven more by the fact that I was expected to drop everything in my life, everything I had going for me… again, or if it was the kind of anger, embarrassment, and feeling of helpless vulnerability you get when someone sticks their foot out and trips you just like he tripped you yesterday in the same spot at the same time, and your helpless little self fell for it again. It must have been a little of both, but more because I felt like I was being picked on by a bully - a bully to whom I was defenseless. He would laugh in my face as he pushed me down over and over. I really just wanted to sit by myself in a corner and stare at nothing in particular, like some shameless kid does at his first high school dance when he's absent a date. Just to stare and think, reflect upon how cruel the world was being to me.

• • •

129

The second Dad heard the news of my reoccurrence, he left work and flew from St. Joseph to Memphis. It seemed instantaneous, how quickly Dad showed up. It was like he'd been in the bathroom for a while and just walked out. Some say time flies when you're having fun. It also does when you're dealing with something catastrophic.

The whole time all I could think about was how mad I was, how much I wanted to shoo it away like a rude fly. But at the same time, I had no idea what I was up against. Medulloblastoma kills if it returns. What could I do but just take it, just bite my lip and take whatever they did to me. I would just suck it up and try as hard as possible not to die. I know now that it's much more than just a physical battle. Or was I up against God? Two worthy opponents that were beyond me - and I was just Johnny, a vulnerable human with clenched fists, a strong heart, and buzzing ears.

· · ·

Dad explained his long talk with Gajjar. "It is best, Rocky, to send John to a hospital in New York City. As opposed to four separate rounds of low-dose chemotherapy with bone marrow support in between, Memorial Sloan Kettering Hospital in New York will do one bone marrow transplant, giving him a very high dose of chemo for a single time only, basically all four rounds and more at once. In turn, we hope to overwhelm the cancer cells and destroy them completely the first time around. The honest truth Rocky, as of this date statistics say that roughly one in five children survive this treatment. Their bodies simply can't take the heavy amount of chemo, and their blood cells become obsolete. However, without treatment, he would surely die. There's really no other way. The new cancer would quickly take over his body. It is important that you inform John of these risks."

It must have been an hour and a half, because I had been asleep in the couch/chairs for 30 minutes or so, but I sat awake waiting for

130

an entire hour, staring at nothing in particular. Mom had to remove me from her lap and join Dad and Gajjar.

Finally, it was my turn. "Your tumor has grown back John," Gajjar spoke in his fast and heavily accented voice. " Fortunately, it has come back in the same spot as before, which is quite a miracle for you John. Your previous protocol did not work as well as expected. Now, we aren't left with much choice. The thing to do now would be to surprise the cancer cells with one heavy dose of chemo. However, we think it is best for you John, to go to a hospital in New York City – one of the few hospitals where they are doing this treatment - to be treated with this high level of chemo. Then you will come back to Memphis for six weeks of radiation."

Everything had happened incredibly fast. It was almost funny how rapidly my life went from happy and almost normal to back in the cancer world.

New York? New York City? I guess I wasn't really thinking of the fact that this second treatment was likely to kill me. I assumed I had to do it anyway, why not be happy that I was being sent to the most famous city in the world?

It was just like the first time. They did my surgery within the next few days. My whole family was there. The night before surgery, we all hung out in my room at the hospital. My surgery was in Memphis this time, not at St. Jude's, but at a different children's hospital named Le Bonheur. It seemed much smaller. However, there was a special doctor who dwelled within its walls – an indisputable master at pediatric brain surgery. The legendary man held an unchallengeable record like a champion boxer. Word says the guy performs multiple neurological surgeries each day, attacking them with ease. Some say he does them with his eyes closed. The thing is, that this guy's record was near perfect. He cuts away the entire tumor with one swipe, leaving no trace.

His name is Dr. Sanford. The man has a different way of going about the surgeries.

Before, when Dr. Mujica did my surgery, he tried to cut as much of the red jelly away without harming as much of the gray jelly as possible. Even if there were specs of red jelly that could only be removed by taking out some gray, then he would leave it for the radiation and chemotherapy to get. Mujica did the standard for treatment at the time. Dr. Sanford uses a much more ruthless method. He cuts away all jelly, confirming that all red jelly is destroyed and gone, showing no mercy for the helpless gray jelly that might be in the way. I'm sure it's similar to the way a hungry dog assaults his bowl of food, completely oblivious about how messy he gets as long as every last bit is devoured.

Lebohner Hospital failed to impress me though. The only thing I could think of was the fact that I was a St. Jude's customer going to an alternate service, like a traitor shopping at the corporate market across the street from his usual Ray's Grocery.

The hospital was smaller. It didn't look as powerful from the outside as St. Jude's did. I wasn't completely sure if my judgment of the place was because I really didn't like it, or if I was just still blowing off steam for the stubborn cancer in my body. I was confused about that, however, until I met Dr. Sanford. I determined that the tales of him were true. He was too cocky to have nothing to be cocky about. His flawless confidence almost scared me. However, I don't think any of us doubted that he was going to breeze through the surgery perfectly. He talked like he knew his brains; it was apparent he had plenty of his own as well.

I was no novice myself. As an experienced brain surgery patient, I wasn't scared stupid like I was the first time. Despite the uncomfortable IV and the ticking sounds of saline and other fluids pumping through from the hanging bags, I had no trouble sleeping the night before.

The morning of the surgery went by fast. It was only 30 minutes from the time I woke up to the time I was rolled into the operating room. I stayed in a waiting room that was more like an "on deck" circle in a baseball game where the next up to bat prepares. It was a large room with beds and mini hospital rooms inside, divided from each other by curtains. Inside of my mini room, there was a TV in the top corner, and a number of things I

132

found in previous hospital rooms, except everything was compacted together. During my time there, the nurse had me put on a gown of light blue sheet-like material that exposed my butt and entire back. Also, I had to wear a blue shower cap. She hooked up my IV to some strange liquid that I think drugged me a little so I would be halfway groggy and delirious when they rolled me into surgery.

The whole family stood around my bed: Mom, Dad, Kristin and Casey, who had come up a few days before. This is where they said their final goodbyes and cast their last lines of encouragement, "You're going to do great John." "Let's say a prayer before they wheel you in." *Sure…*

Everything from that point on went too fast. The nurse busted through the curtains. "Are you ready John?" It was no question, but a command, an order. A last kiss from Mom on the forehead, and before I knew it, I was glancing over my shoulder to see my tearing family wave good luck as the nurse quickly wheeled me up to the tall double doors labeled "SURGERY." I felt like an emergency patient on one of those cheesy hospital drama shows, being rolled quickly around by some nurse who cared more about the rumors of her anesthesiologist lover sleeping with the nurse practitioner than the patient in front of her.

The atmosphere instantly turned white upon entrance - not completely white, but extremely bright like the lights at the set of Cider House Rules. The nurses and doctors were all white with light-blue shower caps on. My mobile bed stopped next to a larger bed, which was obviously the operating bed because the giant and intimidating tools and machinery used to get inside people surrounded it. They more or less dumped me onto it like I was in a dump truck. "All right John, if you can just kind of… roll onto that bed right there…" It seemed people were running around frantically like they had all temporarily misplaced their purpose.

Everyone was doing different things, and each one often came by and hooked something up to me. I wanted to say, "Nope, sorry, the last person beat you to it and already hooked that one to me…" I didn't see Dr. Sanford until the very end. He walked in like he was in a hurry, like he was doing a side chore. At least that's the way it seems whenever someone does something over and over and finally it just looks easy. Like a magician, it was all second nature. His swiftness in moving about and grabbing things was well-organized. He wore blue scrubs, a blue mask over his mouth and a blue shower cap. His short words were muffled behind his mask.

"Hey John, how yah doin'?"

What the hell does it look like? "Good, thanks."

I saw a different man fumbling with the bag at the end of my IV tube. He was sticking a needle into the tube. It was filled with that milky, glueish white stuff. I rapidly darted my eyes like a frantic bird as people ran around me, all wearing masks over their mouths. I noticed Dr. Sanford standing a few feet away talking with one of the other masked creatures. I looked back at the white goopy fluid that was now traveling up the tube into my IV. *This is it...* I tried to fight it. But I knew vey well what I was about to feel. The second it reached my arm and entered my bloodstream, a heavy tingling sensation rushed into my head. My world slowed. I tried to flex my muscles to stop it. Everything started to go white. I was losing control. I continued to dart my eyes but they slowed too. With every split second that passed, I felt multiple bottles of hard liquor pouring into me. The tingling grew heavier. The sound of rushing water filled my head, and the same thousand needles from before hit the floor. Everyone turned white. Dr. Sanford was leaning over me, looking right into my eyes.

• • •

Though a dreamless sleep, the frantic events leading up to my induced slumber were accompanied by a strange confidence. I had done it before, and I wasn't scared this time. I didn't have any control over what was happening, but more a sense of stability, awareness, and acceptance. I'd say something was different about the second time I was put to sleep. I felt prepared… ready for the scalpel, ready for the battles.

11
New Yorker

June, 2000

"24 hours?" It seemed like a ridiculously long trip, but that's how long the road trip from St. Joe, Missouri to the legendary Big Apple was. It was hard to believe that I was really going there. *New York...* it was a fabled land that danced far away in the untouchable dimensions of movies and television.

This time it wasn't just Mom, Kristin, and I. Dad and Casey dropped what they were doing, and my entire family filled the Jeep as we were flying up the highways to America's biggest and craziest city.

Despite the long trip, I enjoyed the free time to let my mind wander. I liked to think of the video games I played throughout my childhood: Mortal Kombat, or Street Fighter II. In fighting games like these, two warriors would meet each other in a battle to the death. The winner of two out of three fights won the battle. At each round, the narrator would kick off the fight with a fiery, demonic shout, "Round 1, Fight!" The battle was between malignancy and me. I had won the first round.

"Round 2... Fight!"

Growing up, I was also a huge fan of the Ninja Turtles. My favorite was Michelangelo, of course. In the first feature-length Ninja Turtles movie, the turtles battled their nemesis, The Shredder, and defeated him in the end. However, in the second movie, which released a few years later, The Shredder came back as Super Shredder: bigger, faster, and stronger.

With five people stuffed in a four-seater Jeep for 24 hours, the trip was hectic, but our long road changed one day into the outskirts of the notorious New York City. *So it does exist...* We slowly approached the skyline that seemed closer and closer, but still so far away. It was like coming upon a mountain range. We had to pass through a giant tunnel to get into the city, the Lincoln Tunnel.

The Lincoln Tunnel, constructed in the 1930's, is three giant tubes of traffic that run 1.5 miles beneath the Hudson River. It connects Weehawken, New Jersey to midtown Manhattan, and bears nearly 120,000 vehicles a day. The enormous entrance surrounded by high, thick stone walls closing into the tunnel, stands as the gate to the great city.

The ten lanes of traffic we drove through started to narrow as we neared the tunnel, and we slowed at an incredible rate. Six of the lanes ended within 200 feet. There had to be a hundred cars and trucks trying to cram into the same space. Horns went off like dogs barking at a vet, and fingers flew like birds.

Lexington Avenue and East 73rd Street, Manhattan... it was our destination that was somewhere within the endless heap of urban jungle. Supposedly, it was where the Ronald McDonald House dwelled. All over the country, near large children's hospitals, Ronald McDonald houses stand for the purpose of courteously housing patients and their families who have to travel great distances to be treated.

Driving through the metropolitan mist of Manhattan to find the place was a long enough distance for me. Bumper-to-bumper traffic moving five miles an hour, with stoplights that seemed to last five minutes at each turn was quite a new experience - hours of new experience in fact.

As we trekked deeper and deeper into the city, shivers of awe ran through my body at the thought that I was finally in New York. I had heard about it everywhere and I had seen it on television and in movies.

The Ronald McDonald House... It was much taller and skinnier than I imagined. There is a Ronald McDonald house in Memphis next to St. Jude's Hospital. It is a free-standing building in the middle of a large, flat yard.

I expected the one in New York to be similar, but it was stuffed between about 50 other 20-story buildings bearing the same archaic cracks and texture like old public libraries. It seemed there were almost too many windows, and they appeared to be strangling the building like vines. Behind one of them was a single bedroom for Mom, Dad, my two sisters and I to live inside until I was done with cancer for good, or at least until it was done with me.

...

The New York Ronald McDonald House is about five blocks away from Memorial Sloan Kettering hospital, where I was to receive my special protocol of chemotherapy.

The day after we arrived, we walked over to the hospital for the first time as an entire family - all five of us, marauding through the streets of New York, ready for the final battle. Like a boxer skipping through the crowd up to a sold-out title fight, with supporting hands holding his shoulders from behind, my family was surrounding me.

New York is an extremely beautiful place. With the small triangles of grass at seemingly every other block, elaborate fountains, and rows of trees in big, square stone pots along the sidewalks, the fine mix of just enough nature into the well structured city blocks made for a super pleasant and exciting atmosphere to walk through. Manhattan was so manicured in some parts, like one big urban-style nursery. Despite all of the stories I had heard, (mostly from watching too much Ninja Turtles who fought an overload of crime in New York City) I felt completely safe, as if the tall buildings surrounding me were guardians keeping watch.

There was never a car-length of open space on the pavement. Every minute of the day, cars and trucks covered the streets like a row of ants on a sugar-covered windowsill. The sidewalks were just like the hallways at my middle school and high school, cluttered with wanderers going every which way. Strangely, the incredible population of foot and street traffic gave me a sense of privacy. I felt like there were so many people out doing their own thing that I was really by myself with my family. It didn't seem anyone else cared, as far as the presence of others... but if something happened, there were hundreds of people seconds away to help.

On each block, there were at least two street vendors selling cold or hot beverages, discount clothing, or household appliances. There seemed to be at least six or seven restaurants on each block, as well as newspaper stands, shops, general stores, banks, cleaners, mailboxes, fashion stores, and most living necessities a person could ever want. Above all of the commercial life on the ground level, the buildings looked like residential apartments ascending to the sky like trees in a thick forest all reaching to get closer to the sun. *Most things anyone would need to live a whole life are within two or three blocks...*

Memorial Sloan Kettering... *There it is...* Despite my excitement to stand before yet another hospital, I did experience a small shiver in my body when I first saw the building. I get a shiver when I hear about something for a long time that is so far away, then I travel great lengths and eventually find myself standing in front of the destination. It's like a fabled legend come true.

● ● ●

"JOHN CATHCART... JOHN CATHCART." *Aw... finally. Something I'm familiar with.* We had been sitting in these bluish chairs in the waiting room for almost an hour. I could hear Gajjar's rapid voice, "When you get to Sloan Kettering John... you are going to find a good friend of mine, Dr. Ira Dunkel. He is the doctor who will be supervising your treatment there."

"John Cathcart?" Some lady peeking from a closed door had called for me twice already. "Dr. Dunkel is ready for you. You can come on back."

"Well Hello! I am Ira Dunkel." Mom and Dad introduced themselves. Dunkel turned to me, "… and you must be John. Am I correct?"

"Hello," I said.

Dr. Ira Dunkel was an extremely kind, small, gentle, and soft-spoken man. He wore big glasses, and had dark hair fluffing out the sides of his head that was bald in the middle. We small talked for about ten minutes. He told us about living in New York - good jazz bars, movie theaters, and places to eat. Then he gradually changed subjects to get down to business. "So John, you probably would like to know what we're going to be doing to you?"

Although he was soft-spoken, he sounded smart, and he was confident in his words. "Well, the first thing we're going to do John, is put in a line." The second I heard the word "line," I involuntarily covered up my chest and quivered. "I bet you had one when you were in Memphis, but this is going to be just a little different. It will be a little bigger, and more rigid. This line has a ring at the insertion point so that your skin will grow to it and the tube will not come out easily." The bullet-shaped scar in my chest from the previous line began to glow with painful memories as he spoke. "After that, we are going to give you about a week to recover from the insertion of your line and your recent surgery. During that week, we are going to put you through several tests, MRI's, CAT scans, and stuff like that; I'm sure you've had a million. When you are done with the tests, and we think you are physically ready, then we will start the bone marrow transplant." "Now, blah blah bleh blah bleh, so bla bla bla." I gazed off for a few minutes, and then caught myself, like so many times in algebra class. "We are going to give you a special medication that will cause stem cells to evacuate your bone marrow and move into your blood stream. Once there, we can easily harvest them from your blood through a filtering process and store them in a freezer to use during your chemotherapy.

The next day, we will start the chemo. At St. Jude's, you received four low-dose rounds of chemo separated by two weeks of recovery and a bone marrow transplant for each round. Since that strategy did not work so well, considering the tumor re-growth, we are going to use a different method. Instead, we are going to give you one single round of chemo that is very strong. In fact, this chemo is nearly ten times as strong as your last chemotherapy dose. We will give you the chemo on one day, one big day of chemo, and then you will stay at the hospital so we can monitor you for as long as it takes you to recover, which may be about two months. We will be watching you extremely close, John. We will watch for your blood counts to hit nearly zero; this is when we know chemo has killed everything, hopefully including the cancer cells, which will be about three or four days after the chemo. Right when that happens, we will quickly give you back all of your stem cells through your line. The goal here is to surprise the cancer cells and completely wipe them out in the first blow, so they don't have time to defend or recuperate."

"Now, it is very important for you to fully understand the risks that are involved with this type of treatment. This is an extremely strong dose of chemo, and if not under the closest supervision possible, it could very easily kill you. The chemo itself is strong enough to do the job, but the highest risk of death will come in the days after chemotherapy, because your immune system will be very low. If you get an infection, even infections normal people get everyday, then your body could do absolutely nothing." *Normal people...* "But John, this is why you will be under constant supervision – under the best medical care in the world. You will have to be completely isolated. People can come in your room, but they will have to wear special clothing to do so. We will be watching you 24 hours a day, making absolute sure that you are completely infection-free. We will provide your every need and want until the day you are physically able to walk out of here. Are you with me so far?"

"Yes," I said. Though I actually faded off again when he had said ten times as strong.

"There are going to be three different types of chemo," Dunkel continued. "I think it is important you know and understand exactly what we are going to give you. They are all three clear

141

fluids formed from dissolved powder. The first and most common type of chemo drug we will give you, is cyclophosphamide. Cyclophosphamide is used in most chemo protocols. It is a drug that acts directly on the DNA. Upon arrival in your body, it causes breaks in DNA strands and abnormal base-pairing, all of which prevents the cancer cells from duplicating because they might be cancerous." *So...* "This is the drug that will cause your hair to fall out. It will make you feel nauseous and make you lose your appetite. It is also known to cause infertility. *Hmmm... why is he telling me this... I'm definitely not being won over...* "Yep, this sounds like the drug for me!"

"Vincristine and Cisplatin are the two other types of chemo drugs you will be receiving. These drugs may cause bruising, maybe bleeding around the body, cases of anemia, constipation, numbness, cramps, and Cisplatin has been known to damage hearing, cause diarrhea, and affect kidneys..." *Oh my God!* It was like he was lighting me up with a machine gun, and each syllable out of his mouth were a series of bullets jolting my body hundreds of times over.

· · ·

July, 2000 – New York City

The same headache that had been stomping around for the past several days continued to knock on my skull, aimlessly looking for a way out like a fly in a closed window. The feverish knot behind my eyes kept me from turning them. Instead, I turned my head to see my mom sleeping awkwardly positioned on the cot next to my bed. I could tell by the slight slant of her eyebrows that unhappy dreams roamed in her stressed mind. The unfortunate moment had been eating away at her mentality.

It had been nearly two weeks since they injected me with the super chemo, and about a week since they gave me my stem cells back. My counts were still at zero. The rest of my family had slept at the Ronald McDonald house the previous night. They needed a good sleep every so often, and the hospital chairs weren't the best for them.

The morning progressed. It was 9:30. Mom sat on a chair buried in the pages of a book. Every time I saw Mom with a book, it was a different book. Since we came here, it's like she started them but couldn't think right, and she gave up after the first 30 pages. Books, at that time, were mere objects to get her through the moments, not personal entertainment as they usually were.

I pressed the button on my bedside remote to raise my head and turned on the TV with the same finger. *Looney Toons...* Elmer Fudd crept through the woods on the hunt for ducks. With a slow steady walk, he turned his big bald head with each step, "Here ducky ducky duckies..." A mother duck drifted across a pond nearby as five little ducklings happily followed. Elmer eyed them from behind a tree and struggled to find a steady aim at the kid ducks, who swam in a figure-eight pattern behind the mother. He eyed the ducks carefully, crouching closer and closer toward the water. He then realized that the mother duck was gone. His confused head popped up. The mother duck was suddenly standing behind him and grabbed the gun. She twisted it into a bow, wrapped it around Elmer's neck into a bow-tie, and pushed him into the water. The duck's lunatic laugh stuck in my head as I turned off the television. Watching it burned my eyes. However, staring at the ceiling too long would as well.

Wha... I couldn't think. I had nothing to think about; nothing to hope for, nothing that I hadn't already hoped for, that seemed worth hoping for anyway. *I could stare at the ceiling more...* Not that I thought if I stared long and hard enough then I would eventually burn a hole through it and escape, but the ceiling was where my mind went when it was blank.

The quiet room was so still. The wall was so bare, with nothing but some pictures of dancing clowns. There were the medical tools behind my head. Sometimes they were interesting to look at, hanging silently and awkwardly shaped like wise sculptures. Each of them had their own special ability or superpower like a band of heroes.

The ophthalmoscope, which is used to look into the back of the eye, hung from a hook as lifeless as a dead man on a noose. It is shaped like the rubber hammer used to test reflexes, similar to a tomahawk. It's head is an extremely narrowed magnifying glass with a light at the tip. Doctors use this to look directly into the pupil. They would get very close, suspending themselves kissing distance to my nose, gazing deep into my eye through the tomahawk. When a doctor looks through the pupil with the lighted magnifying glass, he/she can see inside a person's head. A nurse examined me with the ophthalmoscope once during my chemo and could tell that I once had "beautiful blond hair" by observing the surviving hair follicles inside my head… or so she claimed. However, the reason for the tool is to directly see a blood vessel. They study the vessels in the eye to see if they look diseased or abnormal in any way. If they are in the eye, other vessels throughout the body probably are too.

Right next to the ophthalmoscope was the otoscope, hanging like the convicted partner that was strung up on the same branch. It is also shaped like the tomahawk hammer for testing reflexes. Comparably, the otoscope is a narrowed magnifying glass with a light at the end. It is narrowed at a point like the others so that it can fit deep in the ear drum. It helps to diagnose conditions where a person cannot hear well or certain upper respiratory conditions and sinus problems.

The third hanging tool was the rubber hammer. It's used to test reflexes in order to make sure nerves are working right. The doctors hit you in the knee with it, the Achilles' tendon, the bottom of the foot, and on the veiny side of the elbow.

The next item in the row of tools hanging on the wall was a sphygmomanometer. Some people like to call this a blood pressure cuff. The sphygmomanometer goes around the upper arm and is pumped full with air. This momentarily cuts off blood circulation. As soon as the blood forces its way through, it makes a booming sound. The doctor/nurse slowly releases the pressure off the cuff and listens intently for the level of the booming through a stethoscope. This sound is the systolic blood pressure. When the blood stops booming through, then the vessel is completely open. This is the diastolic blood pressure. The cuff is connected to a gauge that records the pressure. Blood pressure is normally expressed as systolic over diastolic and is measured in units of millimeters of mercury (a standard measurement unit of pressure).

Despite my pain and hunger, my sleeping mom, and my hurling bowl, the instruments that so innocently hung on the wall were my only comrades in that room.

...

Think of a time that you drank alcohol until you passed out. The next morning, you find yourself in bed at a friend's house, or in some totally unexpected spot. The entire previous night is blank in your mind. You were there, and your friends know what you did, but you have not the slightest clue. If this has never happened to you, then think of when you fall asleep. You never know exactly when you make the transition from awake to sleep. It just happens unconsciously. My experience with chemotherapy in New York City was very similar. These memories hold by far the most horrific and graphic experiences of my life that were apparently too heavy for my mind to comprehend at the moment.

I have a jumbled collage of vivid experiences that are organized randomly in my mind. I had others tell me what happened. I really believe chemotherapy in New York City was the closest to death I have ever been - both physically and mentally... closer than when my first tumor was dangerously near success at squishing my brain. I will always remember certain moments during chemotherapy in New York City, because these are the moments that made me. These are my darkest moments ever, and I believe it can take the darkest moments to ignite the light in someone, bringing them to their brightest.

12

Memorial Sloan Kettering Hospital

August, 2000

The chemo experience was similar to what I had in Memphis, only more intense. Days passed under my awareness as a result of my broken mind. The walls of my little room bore an almost hypnotic array of blue and gray dullness that seemed to reassure me I was indeed losing sanity. Similar to the Chinese water torture where the drops hit your face so many times it starts to drive you crazy, the repetitive stillness of the room seemed to waver in and out like the pendulous swing of a grandfather clock.

The slow tick of the liquids from the many bags of chemicals pumping into my line had settled into one chorus, like the millions of crickets at night who form a single orchestra. The medical tools lined the wall behind my bed like ancient novels line the walls of haunted libraries, sitting forever, weathered deep with memories of generations upon generations. The TV was propped up in a corner on the ceiling just as it was in every hospital room I found myself in. It just sat there, tempting me to turn it on and lose myself in its seductive powers.

My family was always there, at least in the room attached to mine. My blood counts had been mostly wiped out by the chemo, and my immune system was more or less obsolete. Therefore, anyone who came into my room had to wear a mask, a shower cap-like hat, and a robe - all composed of this yellow synthetic sterile material that gave anyone a frightening alien appearance. If I ever left my room, I would have to wear the yellow fibers as well. So my family had a small room to themselves that was blocked off from mine with a wall and a giant window. They didn't have to wear the yellow suits in there.

Mom read a book and Dad slept on her lap. Usually, I would have wanted to be in her lap as well, but for the first time in my life, some strange desire for something greater fogged any want for my parents. There isn't any difficult time I experience where I don't want my parents' comfort. However, I didn't at that

146

moment. I didn't want my friends back at home. Being normal wasn't on my wish list right then. I didn't want a nurse. The thought of floating off my bed with more morphine didn't sound exciting either. I was hot, almost sweaty. I still had the thin hospital gown rolled halfway down my body, exposing the crater-covered bony flesh with a greenish tint that was apparently supposed to be my skin. I could see the outline of my ribs like a starving child in one of those *adopt-a- third-world-country-child* promotions.

It was early evening. I was observing the dimming Manhattan atmosphere outside the tiny window.

"There were 25 IV bags at the same time John…" Mom refreshed my memory. *"I counted them over and over."* Each bag attached to tubes and created a series of tributaries into my line. There were bags full of antibiotics, vitamins, various pain medications, morphine, saline, heparin, juices, steroids, and all sorts of medications to keep me from developing any and every kind of sickness while my immune system was at such a low point.

It was well into my stay at Memorial Sloan Kettering. The phrase "broken heart" is often used in love stories. But it can be broken in many other ways… my heart and my mind were in pieces. Just as if a lover had betrayed me, all hope and logic seemed to betray me. I had been in the same room at Memorial Sloan Kettering for two and a half weeks straight. The nauseating reappearance of every single moment had eaten away at me. I had been active most of the day, hurling on and off, stepping out of my bed to the plastic toilet conveniently right next to me because I needed it so often. It was similar to a baby training toilet. I'd sit on the little plastic toilet seat staring at my pitiful skinny legs. Chemo destroyed every hair on my body - my legs and my nuts, bare like a child's. The sight of my droopy, bald sexual organs only reminded me of the fact that treatment would likely destroy any hope of one day producing children. A naked, completely hairless, skinny fifteen year old slumping over a plastic toilet… that's all I was.

It didn't seem worth it to examine or even talk to the gadgets that hung on the wall behind my bed anymore. No matter how intriguing their names or the countless hours of joy they brought me, these material objects no longer satisfied me; they just reminded me that I was stuck.

However, the ceiling, though extraordinarily plain, never seemed to lose my interest. Something about it - so flat, so subtle, but yet clearly above me - suggested that there was something behind it that constantly yearned for my attention, provoking my curiosity. There were times I'd stare for hours and hours that must have passed under my consciousness because I don't remember much else.

. . .

"Coach showed up a little late for practice this morning," Curtis Calloway explained in one of his letters. Curtis would tell me how cross-country's been going in letters he'd send every so often. "Coach Price was there to lead stretches and everything... but when Coach O'Brien did get there, he acted strange. He didn't really say anything to anyone. We did the whistle work out today."

The whistle workout was one of the toughest. That's the workout that grew hair on your chest. The team would split up into about four different groups based on ability, or self confidence. Each group would line up in their masses and one by one, Coach would say, "all right, take off," and the first group, the varsity runners, would go off in a fast jog. About 10 seconds later the next group would take off, then the next, and so forth. Everyone ran around a mile long section of the wooded trail that was shaped like a giant W. Every minute or so, (only he decided when) Coach would blow his whistle. When everyone heard the whistle, they broke out into a sprint. Coach would let everyone sprint for a while, or until he felt like everyone needed a rest, and then blow his whistle again, signaling everyone to shift back to a jog. This would go on for about an hour, and by the end of the workout, most people were spread out either by themselves or with smaller groups - their jog had turned to a ghastly hobble, and their sprint had turned into their original jog. As I remember it, running around and around the big W, I would look up at Coach on the top of a hill with his arms folded, thinking how evil and heartless he looked each time he blew the whistle to make us sprint more. The funny thing is, that's what made us fall in love with him. He was also the one who made us stop, become better runners, and who gave us ice-cold water and popsicles at the end of each workout.

"After the workout," the letter read on… "he was digging around in his truck when we were lining up at his back hatch to get some popsicles. He said he wanted to talk to us about some new uniforms."

The get-well letters came by the hundreds. One specific morning, I was hardly excited to flip through countless letters again as if they were playing cards, each of them expressing the same sympathetic emotions in rather creative ways. I got this one about 20 different times: On the front was an image of a cute dog with its face on the floor. On the inside it read "It's no fun when you're out…" Mostly 75% of the cards I received had sappy images of dogs. Apparently, the general population assumes that hospitalized people enjoy viewing Photoshopped images of dogs. The dogs were nice, but I really wanted a picture of my cat, whom I missed terribly. *Mr. Mischief…* I also got the most cliché message… "Get well soon." However, amongst the pile of get-well letters that morning, was a letter from Coach O'Brien. I rarely got a letter from him. In fact, I don't believe I ever had before. It took all of my energy to muscle open the envelope. I felt inside and pulled out a four-by-six photograph. It was the cross-country team in their new uniforms. They were black, with dark blue and white stripes down the side. Their shorts matched. The front said Central Indians, and on each jersey's shoulder, was a sewn on white patch. It said in bold white letters: "JHP."

Crying is such a strange and interesting thing our body does, it can mean so many things at once. The sight of someone crying can evoke a wave of emotion, good or bad, happy or sad, just like a piece of art can. My tears, at that moment, were sad, angry, and happy all together. Mostly they were sad, because I was missing out. I felt I should be there smiling and being normal and athletic like the rest of them. I was angry at the mysterious evil that held me back, locking me in this far away sterile confinement. I wanted it to be a visible thing so I could punch it in the face. Part of the tears that ran down my cheek and splashed upon the fibers of the letter were happy tears. I was happy because I knew I had a group of real friends that loved me. I was happy because I knew I was not forgotten, which was something I needed to know. Seeing that picture made me think of every other letter and how they all did mean so much to me. I needed to know that people were still thinking of me. I had nothing else to be happy about, and with nothing to be happy about, what's the point of living on? Each and every letter, even the dogs, saved my life. However, this letter made me cry. The group of companions in their new fighting apparel, in their fighting stance, each with my name attached to their shoulders... This carried a deeper meaning than happiness. It wasn't my normal name either. Johnny Hotpants... it was my fighting name; a symbol that classified me as a warrior - missing in action. The picture said more than that I was just missing, but perhaps on a separate mission. On this mission, my fellow soldiers back at home, back in my comfort zone, were behind me.

I decided to write back to Coach O'Brien. I called in my nurse, who I wished was Jennifer from Memphis, and asked for a sheet of notebook paper and a pen. *Coach...I just received your letter and the picture of the team in the new jerseys. That was really awesome. I am angry I am being held back. I am in my hospital room as I write this. It is mostly miserable around here. Chemo is hard; I'm sick, weak, and lonely. Your card made that go away right then. I want to come run more than anything. I don't think I've ever wanted anything so much. Don't count me out this season, because I will come back and compete in a race before it's over. I promise this to you, the team, and to myself. You guys are my inspiration. Thank you.- Johnny Hotpants -*

I didn't show my letter to my parents or anyone. It was mostly driven by the hard emotion of the moment. However, I intended with all my mind and heart to keep my promise to Coach. It wasn't just a promise to Coach and the team, but to myself, and to my enemy. I folded it up and asked my parents to mail it for me.

• • •

Later that night my eyes opened again, and a nurse I'd never seen before came in with a new bag of liquid, the 26th bag. I didn't realize she walked in until she stepped in front of a series of lights from a computer, which made her an unidentifiable silhouette. The bag was a little out of the light, but in it enough that I could see it was a milky blue. Its contents waved at me with ripples as the strange shadow nurse hung the bag. She glanced over and noticed that I was awake and eyeing her movements. Her voice was a soft, angelic, and almost creepy. "This should be the last medication we're going to start you on John. It's called Pervenia. It is going to give your immune system a significant boost that should push you over the top and get you out of here quickly. This bag will drip overnight, and I'll change it tomorrow morning. Do you have any questions?" *Hmmm... with all the strange names of chemos I've had, cisplatin, serotonin... phsyclophosphemed... the name didn't surprise me. What else am I going to say anyway?* "No, I don't think this medicine will be good for me right now."

"No questions, it all sounds good," I said. I just lay still and watched as she took the tube coming from the bag and connected it with the tube coming into my line. I watched with a blank face, like a prisoner on death row who is being hooked up to the chair, straining to show no emotion, but terrified at the same time.

She left the room, leaving behind a grape juice box for me, hoping that I would sip at it but knowing that I wouldn't. The taste... or even thought of something in my mouth produced an awkward gagging sensation. Then I realized that Mom was leaning over my bed in a heavy slumber, gently holding my hand in hers. Dad was behind her with his hand on her shoulder. He was asleep as well. Neither of them had realized that the nurse walked in and talked to me. I could see the hurt behind each of their closed eyes - the pain of not being able to do anything - powerless against such a reckless hate with no face.

• • •

151

Hours passed into the night. Mom and Dad were still half asleep, but they drifted into the adjacent room for sleep without the yellow aprons and masks. I lay alone with the ticking of the bags surrounding me like haunted clocks, staring at the ceiling as if it were sheep repeatedly jumping the same fence; repetitive but mesmerizing. The air was so still as was the cool New York night. The breeze splashed up against my window like a gentle tide against rocks, gracefully wheezing as if it were calling my name. My window was always closed so that outside bacteria couldn't get in.

My spit bowl was nearly full. I kept three or four on a table next to my bed, and I grabbed for a second one. I believed it was the 26th bag's fault - the fact that I was struggling with significantly more saliva than usual. Something from that last bag created this sharp pain in my stomach, as if it were eating away at the tissues. I felt like I'd swallowed several chili peppers whole.

I lay for about 20 more minutes, staring at the ceiling and waiting for the feeling to pass, but it wasn't going away. I knew I was going to hurl soon. I could usually feel it about five minutes before it happened. Just like you can predict a storm from the dark clouds forming, I felt the clouds begin to form in my stomach. But… it would take a while. I couldn't hurl on command, though I would like to have been able to. I usually had to sit and tough it out until things erupted into an actual hurl.

At that point, I sat up in my bed and took deep breaths like I had just woken from a nightmare. Whenever I sat up, a hurl always progressed a little easier. Nonetheless, I still had to wait. I think if there would have been food in my stomach to work with, then the whole process would have gone much quicker, but the fact that it was empty… it's like my body had to search for something else to purge.

The sharp pain in my belly grew. The rest of the room was an audience. The small window, the mysterious bland ceiling, my friends the otoscope and ophthalmoscope, the 26th bag… they were all waiting and staring in anticipation as I was about to perform my feat. I felt a small jolt in my stomach; it was about to come. I properly positioned myself to where I was leaning slightly forward, one hand propping me up on the bed from behind and the other firmly holding the spittoon about a foot from my mouth. The first heave drew on expectantly. I knew exactly how it was supposed to feel for a usual empty-stomach chemo hurl. Nothing came out, but nothing ever did on the first three or four heaves. The second heave came on a little stronger and sooner than expected, but I still considered myself to be undergoing normal hurling conditions.

I waited patiently for the next heave. Several unusual seconds passed, and it became many seconds past due a usual third heave. My mouth hung open, and something seemed to pull at my insides. Then the pain multiplied for a split second. My whole body jolted like I was having shock treatment for a stopped heart. The third heave finally came with a hard sting and it lasted for several seconds. This time, something came out: a long stream of yellowish stomach acid followed by flat clumps, some the size of small pancakes, or McDonald's "McGriddles." The soft, flat clumps in my mouth sort of gagged me in mid-hurl. I knew that they were pieces of stomach lining, because I could feel it, I felt the parade of wasps in my stomach. The pieces were so disgustingly soggy and flat. Landing in my spittoon, they had a strange tan color blurred with a heavy red.

They looked like little graphics on a paper someone had left out in the rain.

I had never experienced this before.

It would have taken me a minute to recover from the shock of the third heave, but a fourth quickly followed with more gagging clumps and more acid that burned the walls of my throat. The fifth heave produced only drips of acid. The climax of the heave lasted even longer than the third. It was like the final heave where everything had to come out because my stomach was about to close up shop, and the employees were taking their time to search under the tables and behind the bar for stragglers. During the climax of a heave when most people hurl, their eyes and mouth are open as wide as possible, with their face stretched like a

153

rubber band. Their neck leans forward so that whatever needs to come out can most easily exit. It is during this moment that the automated position of their body forces one to clearly see the grotesque contents of what has come out of them. I was in mid-climax and the contents I saw inside the spittoon suddenly gave me something to think about other than the fact they were gross. Then, I fell into the moment.

A chill of melancholy emptiness, fear, and hopelessness quickly made its way through all of the nerves in my body - a chill so deafening, so real, that it shattered my heart and mind. I don't think it was solely the soggy chips of stomach lining floating like dead frogs… but simply the passionate shock that things were actually that bad, that hopeless - a complete realization that the enemy eating away at my body was simply and indefinitely beyond me. It was beyond me in a way that no matter how tough I wanted to be, no matter how much a warrior I could have been at heart or mind, no matter how thick the confidence was that I would soon prevail and run a cross-country race, winning over the evils of my life … I just couldn't do it… it was too much. I started to wonder if this was what dying felt like.

That was the first moment I realized how truly alone I was – the moment I was staring in awe at the acidy slates of my stomach floating before me, spitting the pieces out that stuck to the roof of my mouth like cheap potato chips. The incredible weight of the image started to pull me down. My head didn't move, but I felt dizzy as if I were being sucked in to the bubbling pool before me. Then I saw it… it was not necessarily the largest chunk in the bowl, colorful like the rest, but it had a texture. I'd say it was the most landscaped piece, curved and almost rounded off like one would think the insides of a stomach should be. Together, they resembled rolling hills in a storybook… like the giant breasts of the ladies at the front desk in Memphis, or maybe a human butt. Oddly enough, the shape of these strange rejected innards reminded me of the butt chin I analyzed at Westhill Baptist Church years ago.

The wind didn't all of a sudden send any mysterious blow through the window; the door didn't start to flap on its own, nor did my bed raise up and down, but out of the thin air of my empty sterilized world, materialized the voice of the butt-chinned man like Jacob Marley - frighteningly surrounded by Gates and Flames. "In your darkest moments John..." I couldn't stand the pain, not physical, but the pain of total emptiness – something far beyond that of surgery, chemo or radiation. I then knew that I was dying. I quickly tried to accept this, while I waited for the images of my life to pass before me. "In your darkest, lowest moments, just simply reach for the hand of God." The voice rang in my ears. The phrase sounded so ridiculous, so trite and stupid. At the same time, I felt like I had no other option but to just entertain the voice tumbling around in my head.

The peculiar ceiling began to shake violently and pierce its way into my head in sort of an enraged silence. The searing tranquility seemed to crash down on me in flaming pieces, burning away any resistance to hope in the world, any resistance to sanity or logic... My world was an absolute void of nothingness. *This is it. I am leaving this world. I want it to be over so badly.*

I reached out my hands - both of them, to accept what was coming, or where I was going. I grabbed at more than the ceiling, I grabbed for something beyond it with pitiful arms of weakness and defeat. A hand gently slipped into mine like a warm slipper. I did not dare open my eyes, but I looked up somehow, into the light breaking through the dark void of my mind. The grip on my hands was amazingly soft yet firm - firm like something that would never ever let go. The hand was a form of glow pervading down my fingertips and throughout my body. Like Michelangelo's painting of God's infusion of life into Adam on the ceiling of the Sistine Chapel. I could feel the life sparking into every inch of my body. It was a feeling completely inside of me, nothing external, nothing anyone, not even I, could see if they were looking into the room, but a spiritual connection. God was holding my hand.

I suddenly felt at peace. *The truth behind the curtains of Gates and Flames... it is clear now.*

· · ·

"John… John? John Boy wake up. You've been sound asleep all through the night. You haven't slept that good since we got here. Neither Mom nor I heard a sound from you all night." Mom was standing next to Dad, smiling at me. They were proud of me for sleeping. "I'm so happy for you!" she said. I hadn't seen them excited about anything for a long time. "I want you to get up. I have something to show you." Dad said.

Kristin and Casey were both standing in the room with smiles as well. They were each covered with the yellow sterile material. They came to my bed and gave me hugs. "We're going to the physical therapy room down the hall, so you'll have to put on the yellow stuff. Are you up for it?" Dad asked.

There was a physical therapy room nearby; in one of the many hallways on my floor of Memorial Sloan Kettering. It was a large open room set up like an aerobics studio. *Why are they taking me there…* The only reason I could think of was that there was an audiologist office in the corner of the room. The doctor had been asking about my hearing a lot. *They are probably going to test my hearing again.*

Mom held my hand as I hobbled outside. It was the first time I had been out of my room in nearly four weeks. I struggled maintaining balance in my uncoordinated legs. Casey rolled the tall clothes hanger behind me where the bags of fluid hung, still pumping slowly into my body. The 26th bag was gone. She rolled it behind me with such ease and a smile that said she enjoyed helping me. Casey looked like she would make a good nurse, the kind of nurse every patient would like to have. Kristin walked with me on the other side. Mom and Kristin supported me whenever I started to fall.

Dad opened the large double doors to the physical therapy room. I couldn't believe my eyes as the open doorway revealed what was in the room. The sight overtook me, and I thought I would break down in tears, but I was too much in shock.

156

Standing in a large group before me, was the New Generation Singers from St. Joseph, Missouri. A group of about 30 youth and some adults stood there with huge smiles on their faces like when the birthday boy enters the room at a surprise party. The New Generation Singers are a praise-oriented choir that travels around the country singing at churches and schools. I recognized several friends from school amongst the crowd – especially one of my best friends from childhood, Prashak, who situated himself on the front row two people from the left. I remember this exactly.

I couldn't believe it. It was so random, but beautiful, like a...

For once, I couldn't compare it to anything. It was just an amazing, overwhelming feeling of suddenly being blown away with love...

They started singing. They sang these wonderful, happy praise songs. The voices were powerful like a Harlem church choir. As they sang, some stared intently at the director in front of them waving his hands around, but most all of them stared right at me. *The New Generation Singers? In New York?*

I turned back to my family who were also looking at me, smirking as if they had this idea surfacing for quite some time. Their smiles said, "Impressed aren't yah?"

I was embarrassed to be in front of everyone sick, bald, and in a yellow alien suit. Though, as the music went on, and the feeling of gratefulness settled deep in my body and soothed my pain, I began to forget where I was or how I must have appeared. I looked back at my family, still with giant smiles, and Dad raised his eyebrows at me. My expression said "How did you..."
I turned again and caught eyes with Prashak for a second time. He was looking at me too. His brown freckly face circled around his glasses. The way he stretched his mouth as he sang baritone elongated his freckles and cheeks which tilted his glasses up and down. His smile, this time, was personal. He was saying, "Hats off to you buddy."

13
Well, Now What?

I came home in the middle of October. I had started treatment in early July. I miraculously survived the super chemo and then moved back to Memphis, where I lay under the rays of radiation that burned through my brains once more. It caused me to hurl everyday, and that lasted six weeks. During that time, just Mom and I stayed at the Ronald McDonald House. Living in a separate apartment was just too hard and inconvenient for us. The radiation was the same as before, only this time, I had something to look forward to. Most of the other kids at the Ronald McDonald House were very sick and didn't want to hang out or be social at all. So I hung out with Mom, and I prayed. In New York, I learned that prayer helped me escape. Prayer, to me, became like little vacations where I could get away from everything and connect with something beyond the present moment. Prayer brought me to this world of peace that sometimes shut out the physical feelings as well.

I would run laps around the Ronald McDonald House, thinking I would still fulfill my promise and run a race by the end of the year.

Three laps around the Ronald McDonald House was all I could do. That was maybe a quarter of a mile. I would also try to work out. There was actually a small weight room in the Ronald McDonald House that apparently was never used because of the cracking paint on the walls, the few mismatched weights on the floor, a bench, a treadmill, and a broken bike. I could bench press 10 pounds on good days.

I discovered things in a new light as I returned to St. Jude's Children's Research Hospital in Memphis. One of the greatest changes that had been made, was the paint job. The nauseating blend of red and white was no longer the main color scheme. Most of the floors were still white, and the poles that led down the hallways were still red, but every wall was painted with nice cool comfortable colors, such as blue and green, and merging giant murals of basketball players, magical cities, and underwater scenes with mermaids. There were computers set up in the waiting rooms for the kids to play on. Also, the old couch/chairs were gone. They replaced them with softer couch/chairs that had a nice dark blue and green color like the walls. There was a fish tank in one of the waiting rooms, and to my surprise, both waiting rooms were a lot quieter than I had remembered. Some of the furniture was re-arranged, and it made everything just seem a little more intimate.

I started to actually enjoy being back at St. Jude Hospital. It felt more comfortable and more quiet, or… I think I'm going to use the word "peaceful." Discovering this made me realize more and more how St. Jude's saved my life, and how special the place is to me.

While sitting in one of the waiting rooms, I saw another little girl playing with the toys and the magnetic tables with cars and buildings on top. She looked about the same age as the girl from years back, but it was a different girl with probably a different cancer and an entirely different story. She was gluing up a paper on the wall. On it was a sloppily drawn angel, and words in multi-colored letters: "St. Jude's… the place where angels fly."

...

My stay in Memphis was overlapping the start of the school year in September. I wasn't about to miss a year, so I took classes via the Internet. Every day, I would go to the computer room in the Ronald McDonald House and sign onto *Net Meeting* (Google hangouts would come 13 years later.) At school, they placed a laptop computer on the desk where I would have been sitting. The whole screen was my face. I was just there like any other time. The other students could see me, just as if I had evolved into a computer. Or like chemo and radiation melted my body, and all they could save was my brain. So they stuffed my brain into a computer that would be me forever.

159

It was a new challenge for the St. Joseph School District to accomplish, and a groundbreaking idea for education in Northwest Missouri.

Dr. Dunkel said I was one of the fastest ever to come in, survive that level of treatment including the radiation at St. Jude's, and make it out and back to school. I did it all in about three and a half months, and was one of the few cancer fighters my age to stay in school the whole time. The chemo plan was fairly new, and pretty risky, but a few alterations to the protocol saved my life and sent me out the doors in record time. That same protocol will be used much more, always improving, and saving countless more lives of children with deadly forms of cancer.

• • •

October, 2000

Central High School football games are one of the largest weekly events in town. On most nights, it seems half the population of the city is there. In the mountain of bleachers next to the field, you'll find the widest variety of people. Little siblings of players and cheerleaders that run up and down bleachers or on the sides of the track, groups of middle school kids that can't wait long enough before they're in high school and actually have a purpose to be there, the multiple assistant coaches (parents of players), the parents of the dancers and cheerleaders, the teachers, the exalted Central alumni visiting from college, the band members, the nerds, the preps, the jocks, and every other little sub-clique there is clustered together in little sections of the bleachers to signify their presence and stance among the rest of the town. These are the Friday nights where it all happens. The atmosphere is loud, the air is chilly, and memories are in the making.

I had missed about a month and a half of my sophomore year. The life I once had seemed to fall back right in front of me, and I guess I was just supposed to live it like nothing ever happened. I was back in time for fall homecoming. Even those who don't normally come to the games come on homecoming night. This is the night where the government of each of the four classes designs a float and makes a lap around the track during halftime. The crowd cheers as the floats go by, and after that the royal homecoming court is announced and they march down the stairs in their glittering formal outfits.

It was ironic that it was my first day back too. The way I saw it, it was my homecoming night. I was still sophomore class president. I was back to fit in, and I was back to assume my title.

I showed up a little late for the game. Mom and Dad came with me, and they dropped me off in the back of the football stadium by some tennis courts. It was about 8:00 just before halftime; the dark had just settled in for the night. In the parking lot behind the football field, the student government members of each class were scattered around getting their floats ready to parade around the track. My group was standing next to the fence in back of the field making the finishing touches on our float (a glamorous pickup truck decorated with ribbons and Christmas lights). There were nine other people, the elected class treasurer, secretary, and seven student senate members. They had each been good friends to me. It's a strange sight, to see a group of friends you haven't seen for a long time, especially after you've been playing cards with death for several months. The sudden sense of reality is so heavy, like in *Homeward Bound* during the return of the legendary dogs and cat. "Shadow! Chance! Woof Woof!!! Sassy!" It took me a moment to swallow it, and I started walking over. I noticed the way they talked at each other, their adaptive inside jokes, reflexive sarcasm, and guiltless laughter, a way of conversing with genuine friends that I had not experienced for so long.

I imagined my appearance to everyone. The last time they saw me freshman year, I was strong and athletic. During my second battle with cancer, I had lost around 30 pounds. My arms and legs were skinny like sticks. Every hair on my body was completely gone including eyelashes. The complexion in my face wielded an unhealthy lime color. In spite of my physical appearance, I dressed nice, and I didn't cover my bald head with a hat as I had done in middle school. I was ready for the homecoming football game, the big event of the fall. I had on jeans, a white dress shirt, a nice leather coat, and a smile.

"JOHNNY!!!" Claire, the girl elected class secretary, shouted out as she spotted me approaching out of the corner of her eye. She instantly ran over and jumped into my arms. Well... she kind of lifted me up in hers. Brandy, the elected class treasurer, screamed and then quickly added to the group hug, "How are you?!!! Is everything OK? We missed you!!!" The rest of the small group attacked me instantly with questions, concerns, and hugs. "It's great to have you back Cathcart," one guy said to me. He ran against me last year for the position of president. He lost of course, but found himself a seat in the student senate. In my absence, he had assumed the generic role of leader of the sophomore student government; he seemed to be the one directing people around. I talked with everyone for a minute, then the same guy asked as he motioned to the bed of the truck with a smile, "Well, it's almost half time. You ready to hop on and reclaim your throne?" I glanced over to the stadium and watched the crowd roar as the pom-pom girls finished their dance number and started leaving the middle of the field. I got goose bumps. It was time for the floats to make their way around the track and for the royal coronation.

Everyone of us hopped into the bed of the truck and prepared for the ride, grabbing bags of candy and things to throw into the crowd. One of our teachers was in the driver's seat, the faculty sponsor for the sophomore class officers. The truck jolted forward and pulled up to the track. We stopped before it and watched the freshman go around first. We were second, then the juniors and seniors. The band marched onto the field. The typical clanging drums and horns filled the atmosphere as the freshman truck made its way around the track. It really was a mountain on the other side. The bleachers spanned the length of the football field and were well over half of one tall; they were packed. I tried to imagine what people would think when they saw me. I didn't tell anyone I was coming home.

It was soon our turn to go. Slowly and glamorously, we rolled out to the track. As we made our way around the first turn, coming upon the bleachers, we started unloading the bags of candy and launching them into the crowd. We were close enough to everyone that I started spotting faces in the crowd. Some people started to recognize me and point. The thunderous crowd was powerful, and time seemed to slow. In the distorted slow motion, I tried to swallow the reality of all these people in front of me, all these friends I had left behind. Hundreds of people were going crazy. Girls screamed. Guys laughed and fought over candy.

I noticed Taylor, who had known I was coming back and was expecting me. Mom and Dad sat in the back with their friends, everyone waving and cheering like happy zombies. I recognized several teachers as they seemed to lose any sense of self-control they had inside the classrooms. Everyone was jumping and yelling, creating this massive, hazy swarm of bees. Everyone on the floats were going nuts too, launching entire bags of candy into the crowd like candy-grenades. I noticed a group of people toward the side of the bleachers that weren't all going nuts. It was the JROTC, the army guys. A few of them were cheering and catching candy. I recognized Jerry, the guy from freshman English. He was hollering and throwing out his arms, but there was one guy next to him who caught my eye. In all-out uniform, he stood completely still, like he was keeping guard of something. *He must have done the flag and national anthem ceremony at the beginning of the game.* He caught my eye because he was staring right at me. The guy was beefy and big. We were about 20 feet away from the bleachers and he was about the seventh row up and to my right quite a bit, but somehow, all the way from the moving float on the track, with the eyes of hundreds weighing upon me, this guy's presence seemed to leap out and grab me. He looked familiar. Surely our eyes met for about three long seconds. I shook off his glare and continued to throw candy out.

We finished our lap and pulled into the parking lot by the tennis courts. I stood on the truck for a couple seconds after people hopped off and looked back at the football field, the crowd, and behind that, the practice football field, the long front yard of the school, and finally the massive brick building. The huge complex looked like a castle fortress from far away. The lights from the stadium illuminated the daunting campus to make it look powerful and Transilvania-like. I looked back at all of my friends in the bleachers, the entire high school. It was time for me to get back to where I left off. Only now, after missing out on a year and a half of school, I believe I had grown and matured in my own ways. *I am ready. It is time. Well, that is, if they are ready for me.* I debated in my mind for a minute whether they would take me back as "Johnny Cathcart," or as "the kid who had cancer." I didn't want a special status at all, just complete normalcy. However, I didn't know if that was possible. Brandy called back at me "What are you doing Johnny?" motioning me to follow the group back to the bleachers. I hopped down, feeling a sudden rush of confidence. *All right, this is it. Let's go be normal.*

14

Central High School, First Day Back

"Hey Hotpants!" Ben, a varsity cross-country guy said to me when I first walked in the side doors of Central High School. The doors were on the Southwest wing of the school near Coach O'Brien's room. It was one of the less heavily populated entrances to the school during mornings. It was my first day back, and the last thing I wanted was to get mobbed by hugs and kisses from people that were either my friends, claimed to be my friends because they felt bad, or because they wanted to impress others by letting them all know that they were friends with the cancer kid.

"Hotpants! Glad to have you back!" said another girl that walked behind him. I don't think I knew this girl. *Well, so I wasn't Johnny, or the kid with cancer… they all seemed to acknowledge me as Hotpants…*

"Cathcart?" *I'd recognize that squirrelly voice anywhere…*
"Twombly!" I shouted. He was one of my very best friends from years before. Back in the eighth grade, we'd take my parents' analog video camera and shoot short movies with inside jokes and stupid characters. We were responsible for such classics as *The Exorcist 2, The Mad Urinator Strikes Back,* and *The Return of Fluffy* (the chilling epic about the ghost of a friend's dead rabbit).
"How are you dood?" he asked. We had our own way of spelling dude… "*dood."* We could type it faster online, and we'd know it was each other talking whenever we saw it.

"Twombly!!! I am excellent! What is up my friend?"

"Oh you know… You look good."

"Hardly, but thanks dood. So what did I miss out on?"

"Not really… nothing's been going on. Everyone's just been waitin' for you to get back, yah know." We were being pushed away from each other by the crowd. "We'll make lots more movies this year, good times?"

"Yeah yeah – good times." I said back as we shook hands right before we were pulled apart.

The very next person I ran in to was Mary McClure, a freshman who I'd not seen in years. She hit me from behind with a fierce hug. Mary and I were next-door neighbors growing up. We used to play basketball as little kids, and wait at the bus stop together every day.

My family had bought our new cat, Mr. Mischief, when I was about seven. It was a cool October day and I was a little late getting ready. "John! Hurry up, you're going to miss the bus!" Mom hollered from downstairs in the foyer of our giant old house. The sound of her voice echoed through the large rooms when she yelled from the foyer. I ran downstairs to meet her. She presented me with my backpack and opened the door, motioning for me to hurry down to the bus stop by the street. I noticed Mr. Mischief had joined us, rubbing and purring at our legs. "Have a good day sweetie!" As I started down the porch steps and the long driveway, I could see young Mary McClure at the stop waiting patiently for the bus, and for me, her bus stop companion.

The big yellow bus was already coming down the street and slowing by the time I got halfway down the driveway. I looked behind at Mom and saw that Mr. Mischief had been following me. He could only go so fast, and I was running by now. Mary had already stepped aboard when I got down to the stop.

I stepped up into the yellow bus and gave my morning salute to the old wrinkly driver. When I started down the aisle to find my seat, I noticed the kids were all looking out the window towards my house. "OH MAN, LOOK AT THAT FAT CAT!" Some loud freckle-faced boy shouted. "WHOA, THAT'S CATHCART'S CAT!" announced another one. Instantly I felt a warm wave of embarrassment rush through my face. I looked back to my driveway and lo and behold, there was my precious, incredibly plump cat sprawled out innocently in the middle of the driveway next to the bus stop, staring happily up at everyone in the bus, posing like a supermodel.

Every time I see Mary McClure, I think of that moment. I will always give tribute to that moment as being responsible for my cat's fame.

"John! How are you!" "Johnny!" "John!" "Cathcart?" "Hotpants!" "Johnny!" "Hotpants!" "Cathcart!" "Johnny boy!" "Johnny!" Within the next six minutes between the moment I walked in the back doors to the dramatic final stretch to my first-hour class, I was bombarded by hundreds of loud greetings. Many of them were good friends. They called me by all sorts of different names as if I had signs of them posted on my back. About 30% of them, however, were people that had either never talked to me before, or that I had never seen in my life.

There it was, just down the hall and on the left: the first classroom I've been in since the whole mess. The final trudge to my classroom was like fighting my way to the end zone in a football game without a blocker in front. The loud commotion from the hallway seemed to get sucked away as I quickly opened the door and stepped inside the room. Mrs. North, the instructor for Medieval History, was leading a conversation with the 25 students already sitting at their desks in the classroom. The second my foot hit the ground inside, the laughter immediately stopped and everyone turned right to me. The door behind me shut with a thunderous boom. I think a whole three seconds of pure silence passed before someone spoke, like I was some wanted bandit who just stepped into a whisky bar.

"Well, Mr. Cathcart?" Pause... "Welcome back!" Mrs. North continued in a delighted tone. I glanced around at all the eyes still fixed on me - many smiling, many indifferent, some staring stupidly because other people were looking and they had no idea who I was. I bit my lip, took a step forward, and played along.

"Mrs. North! How you doin'?" I went up and gave her a big hug like it had been forever since we'd seen each other. I thought it was the appropriate thing to do. After exchanging dubious small talk with North and answering for her the ultimate question "Are you feeling alright," I turned to find a place to sit. I noticed the empty desk where the computer sat during my *Net Meeting* attendances. I felt some eyes still on me as I made my way to my reserved seat. *These people have had me the whole time, only I've been a machine. I wonder what they're all thinking; did they like the machine better? Was I a disappointment? Did they expect something greater, a mech warrior still wearing the computer as my head?*

Mrs. North started in, "Well good morning everyone. I'm very happy to announce that Mr. Cathcart is back with us. I'm sure he is delighted as well, right?" She turned to me and said, "Do you feel comfortable Mr. Cathcart?"

"Yeah I'm good, thanks." I responded quickly to move her on.

After a few seconds of silence, her brows rose, her eyes opened wide, and she dove into one of her famous stories that I had heard so much about, and got to see bits and pieces of while in Memphis. Her stories were interesting, but I think what made them famous is the suspicious smile that grew on her face during the awkward pauses. At different points, she would pause and raise the side of her mouth and the brow above it to the same angle to let the weight of her words seep into our minds. It was not long before the rest of the class was deeply engaged in Mrs. North's story about medieval torture involving some hot poker. I unfortunately did not sink into the depths of her story. Rather, I dwelled in the increasing sting during the silent parts. It was the ringing… mixed with the ambient resonant frequencies of every other thing in the room, plus the unnecessary peaking of Mrs. North's sharp voice. Sometimes, I just wanted to throw a pencil on the ground so I could hide under my desk and cover my ears. My ears actually stung.

• • •

After class, the hallway was filling with inaudible noise from hundreds of voices and footsteps. I stopped to think for a minute. *I'm really back in high school. This is not Memphis anymore.* Life had changed so fast. It was like I woke up from an incredibly lucid dream filled with reoccurring characters, feelings, and situations that all connected. Strangely, I remembered it too well for it not to have been real. It just didn't really feel right being back at school, like I didn't belong there. Its like I was visiting an old town I used to live in, but didn't anymore.

. . .

I believe a throat-clearing cough is generally underneath everyone, and that nobody should ever think twice of such a mild form of bodily eruptions. However, after I let out two coughs in the middle of a lecture in eighth hour chemistry, Mr. P felt a need to stop class and make sure that I was all right. "John, are you OK?" I quickly responded, "Yeah I'm good..." I could completely understand people's concern for my health, considering it was my first day back from a second battle with brain cancer, but it was extremely embarrassing to have everyone apparently constantly afraid that I might keel over and die. As I tried to look as normal as possible for the remainder of the class, I felt a sustained abundance of blood sitting up in my face. I noticed my ears ringing loudly again. Sometimes I couldn't even hear Mr. P. *What is going on with me?* I could feel my face was red as a rose the whole time. I could feel everyone's heavy stare melting me down.

The bell rang and I finally got to get up and leave the room. I couldn't wait to get out of that building. Throughout the entire day, I felt so out of place - like I was special - not special like good... special like embarrassing special.

I almost felt like a banished prom date running away from a dance. As I walked quickly down the stairs and through the hallways of school, I tried to keep my eyes on the ground, avoiding anyone who wanted to stop and talk to me. "How is it to be back?" "Are you feeling OK?" "So... is all the cancer gone?"

I parted my way through the crowd of people and finally saw the light of the door to the outside. My pace quickened, my strides expanded... POOF! I got a mouthful of arm! For a split second my face plunged into the cotton t-shirt covering this alien shoulder, I gasped and inhaled the moist sweat-tinged stench of body and, although the unique scent was surprisingly familiar, I gagged slightly. The impact sent me back a few inches and allowed me a glance at the person that ran into me. The moist cotton t-shirt was camouflage. The guy was a little over six feet tall, his shoulders even with my face. He was bullishly built, thick and chesty, and wore blue jeans with black combat boots. Hanging around his neck, was a silver dog tag with a name I couldn't make out. His arms even puffed out a little from his side, not because he was trying to look that, but because the bulk of his muscles actually did push them out. His lightly shaven head complemented its awkward Sloth-like shape. His deep, strong eyes twitched as he turned to catch a glimpse of his convicted bumper. They seemed to cast burning rays down to the ground like a magnifying glass, radiating a fiery aura of intensity.

As he neared the end of his turn and laid eyes upon me, his face softened and his eyes lit up as if he knew me, and was glad to see me. I recognized him. It was Jerry's mysterious JROTC friend from the bleachers.

"Johnny Cathcart." *Oh great, he does know me.* "I'm on my way to after school training. I don't think it's going to be too long."
...*What?* He knew my name, but I had no idea of his. Combining the ill stench that emitted from his shoulder, and the strange first sentence that came out of his mouth, I was already entirely weirded out by this guy. I could tell that he was probably suffering from a slight mental illness or something... so I just played along.

"Woa, all right, cool man."

"Where are you going?" he asked. *Why does he want to know? He thinks he knows me?*

"Oh, I'm just uh, headed home yah know," I responded.

"Where is home nowadays?" he asked.

"Um... well..."

He read the suspicion in my face. "I'm Ford, remember?"
I didn't want to be rude.

"Oh! yeah, of course man."

"Hey, I believe they're needing me," he said. *Oh I'm sure 'they're' just dying...* He seemed to respond to my thought...

"Yeah sure, well it's good to have you back."

"Yeah, yeah it's great. I'll see you later."

He just nodded "Yeah," and walked away. He walked like a general with his chest out, like he had some important job to go accomplish.

I hesitated for a minute after he left. I couldn't believe that guy just randomly talked to me like that. It was almost creepy. Then from the corner of my eye I noticed Mom's car sitting on the street by the school. She was waiting for me. *Well, that was an interesting first day.*

...

"John, dinner's ready!" *Ahh... Something I haven't heard for far too long a time...* The cold wind was already starting to blow and the brown leaves had just started to fall. I'd have to say fall has always been my favorite of the seasons. I loved the smell, and I got to wear my leather coat and scarf. We always had a fire going in the fall. There was always a football game, and a hot drink bubbling with spices. The house was warm with pumpkin spice-scented Yankee candles and cozy Thanksgiving decorations like old corn stalks and smiling scarecrows.

My family had moved over the summer. After many years, we finally left the mansion on Lovers Lane. It would have been very hard on me to leave the house I grew up in, but I was still in

Memphis when Dad and Casey made the move. The giant old house was starting to fall apart on us anyway. Being built near the turn of the century, its strong columns started costing a lot of money to fix over and over.

Spaghetti. Mm – mmmm… I could eat spaghetti for hours… that is, Mom's spaghetti. There is really nothing like it. Though it is made similarly to the way American spaghetti has always been made - long thin noodles covered with a store-bought jar of Ragu mixed with ground beef - Mom always waves her hands over the pot, sprinkling her own magical pixy dust on the taste. The distinctive aroma wafted through the air and flirtatiously brushed my nostrils. Like a dog being summoned hypnotically to a steak, my nose led me from our new TV room, more spacious than the one at Lovers Lane, through the house with my eyes gently closed. I am confident that the scent could safely guide me through a mine field.

"So how was your first week back John?" Dad started up the dinner conversation with the question everyone was waiting for.

"Well, it was alright I guess." I wish I could have responded with such a simple statement as that… like most normal kids, but the week was much more exciting.

"People wouldn't stop hugging me and asking if I was feeling OK." I paused to messily chew my noodles. When my two front teeth chopped through the bundle, the rest of the noodles fell and plopped back on to my plate. There was really no other polite way to eat it. If I tried to roll the spaghetti onto my fork, the noodles would just slip off and hang.

"Teachers were the worst," I said. "In the middle of class they would stop the lecture to check and make sure I was OK - right in front of everyone."

"Oh don't worry about it John," Mom said. "Everyone's just been really worried about you. It won't last for long. Once you get into a more routine schedule, everything will get right back to the way it was before."

Several times throughout the dinner, they asked me whether or not I was hearing them right. "What?" Sometimes my responses were off. My parents talked daily matters. "Is the bread in the broiler done?" Dad asked Mom. *Had the Royals won? They don't usually talk baseball, and they know that I don't really know baseball either, but...* "The Royals aren't playing anymore guys. The season is over." I said. My parents both looked at me and shrugged. They gave each other that look when a baby is noisy in church and the parents are silently debating who's going to take the kid outside.

"You know John..." Dad started, "The chemo was hard on your ears. You're not going to hear that well for a while. It might get a little better over a long period of time once the chemo completely exits your system, and your body has time to fully recuperate, but..."

Of course – I knew it wasn't going to be over that easily. My enemy might have been defeated, but as evil as it was, it left an aftertaste that could still bring me down. It was just like in Lord of the Rings when Gandalf defeats the Balrog, demon of the shadows. As the monster falls into the pit and Gandalf runs away, and the Balrog slings one last whip of evil that pulls Gandalf over the edge. Although gone, the Balrog was not giving up on killing his foe, just like cancer; it does not easily give up.

• • •

Practice was at Central the next day. "Johnny Hotpants Cathcart," Coach said as I walked into his room. He said that every time I entered. "How are yah feeling today?" I talked with Coach for a few minutes, then I watched as the guys jogged out the door behind me and they took off down the street in a pack, the definition of their calf muscles bulging with each stride. The season was almost over, and I was absolutely in no condition to run a race.

173

I needed to run, not only to beat cancer officially – but to beat myself. I needed to become the epitome of tough, not just a sick bald kid whom everyone felt sorry for. I needed to be an example of a normal high school athlete with a normal life and normal problems, but I couldn't. If I tried to run more than a half a mile, I would collapse. My blood counts were still down; they wouldn't be back to normal until the next year. I couldn't run free yet. I watched the runners disappear down the street. The anger I built up all throughout the summer and the passionate rage that kindled inside bubbled up to my consciousness again. I knew it was only a matter of time.

15
Missouri State Cross-Country Championships

Jefferson City, MO, November, 2000

In a big white van, some friends from the team, two of Curtis
Calloway's grandparents, and I rolled east across Interstate 70
from St. Joseph to Jefferson City. The season ended without
mercy to my desires. I had failed my commitment to running a
race by the end, and I'd have to wait until junior year. The rest of
the team had earned first place at the conference meet, they got
second at Districts, and second at Sectionals, thus breaking
through the legendary gateway to State, the final bout for the
championship. Central had made it there before, and they
continually claim the throne as one of the best cross-country
teams in Missouri, just as coach said that first day of practice.
They have never won State before, and that year, we had a team
more equipped with talent and determination than any in Central
High history. So the pressure was on.

As we entered Jefferson City, we could already see the effects of
the meet several miles away from the park where it was
happening. There were cars from all over Missouri crammed
along the streets, creating a line miles back from the park. Traffic
was backed up as far as the eye could see.

Closer to the park, there were school buses crammed in a parking
lot like war aircrafts at an army base, with the troop's name on
each bus. *Hey, there's our bus.* "St. Joe Central." As non-threatening
as the name sounds, it sparks a flush of intimidation among all
competitors. I could hear the different coaches from around the
state as they gawked at the name, "Ahh... so we meet again,
Central Indians. So you think you can outlast my boys this year...
Ha! We'll see about that."

Tents covered the hill behind the marked course, each bearing
their unique fighting colors. There was music blaring through tall
speakers around the park with the hard beat of *Eye of the Tiger*;
typical music for cross country meets. Fans walked around like

lemmings, aimlessly following the people in front of them as teams jogged down the course and around on the grass. Several were at their tent stretching or munching on Power Bars, an untainted focus deep in their eyes. The atmosphere screamed competition. Actually, it was more like a brigade of tiny flies buzzing and screaming the word inside everyone's ear canal.

As we approached our tent, Coach came to greet us. "Great day to run isn't it?" He said. There was already a group of Central guys stretching by the tent. "Guys get unpacked and start jogging the course; get to know every divot in the ground and every little turn. There are unforgiving hills that come up quick on this course." He turned to me. "Johnny HP Cathcart... Glad you could make it." I felt I needed to salute to him like a drill sergeant, but I nodded and shook his hand, glad to be there as well. He shouted out to the guys jogging up to the course, "The gun goes off in one hour and ten minutes, but the girls race starts in 25, so make one lap good enough."

I proceeded into the tent where Peter Fontane was stretching. "Hotpants! Whoa... man, I'm glad you came out to support us." I shook his firm but slippery hand, already perspiring.

"Johnny Hotpants - Glad you could make it." Assistant Coach Roger Price said in his James Taylor voice. "I'm sure it means a lot to the boys. After all, they dedicated the season to you." Fontane left to join the rest of the guys to jog the course. They looked like a pack of sled dogs eager to mush. I was left there to watch, to be another fan, a sideliner who screams his throat dry as the runners pass.

The girls' team also made it to State. I stood with some other team members near the ropes within 200 meters of the starting line waiting for the girls' race to start. The Central girls were already out at the starting line warming up with their form running and last minute stretching. The five-minute gun cracked into the air. Then, as a team tradition, the girls huddled in a group and started praying.

Meanwhile, the starting line was now filled from end-to-end with hearts of athletes ramming against their chests so hard that the

176

ground shook. The girls' race was just about to start. A big round man dressed like a tourist walked out in front of everyone, said some things, and then he blew his whistle and raised his hand, but I didn't hear a thing. I was standing at the side of the course about 200 meters out from the starting line. Crack! The resonance left my ears in the dust as the noise ripped into the silence like a torpedo through water. *I heard that!* It happened so fast, it seemed like the massive army of girls were already closing in. It's strange how this part lasts so long when you're running, but to a by-stander, it's the fastest part.

As the procession of runners flew by, all of the fans were pushed back by a slap of the wind. Towards the front of the mass, I spotted Central's girls. The air was already stuffed hard with roars of loud screaming and rasping that hurt my ears and drowned out any of the puny additions my throat could produce.

Waves of people started darting over to the next part of the course where the girls ran by. Hundreds of parents ran hard, each of them holding up their pants and jeans as they went because of morning dew on the ground. It was nuts, chaos, like a string of firecrackers had just gone off in a cave full of bats. Coaches were waving their hands and clipboards about like wild monkeys as they ran, trying to scream numbers out as they went. I wondered what someone would think if they saw them and didn't know about the meet.

I could only run as fast as most parents or their little kids, which tugged at my heart. I couldn't keep up with my team.

It seemed to go really fast, the entire girls' race. From start to finish, my heart was racing to get from one place to the next, and before I knew it, people were already shouting out, "I heard so-and-so's team all made it in already!" The area near the finish line was packed, and the ground rumbled with the heavy stampede of girls running in. Coaches crowded around the finishing chute with clipboards, waiting to tag runners and scribble down their time as they came by. From what I could see, exhausted girls were already hobbling through the chute with medals shoved in their jelly-like hands.

As I observed before, this is the point in the race where the emotion reaches an incredible extreme, a sort of climax. The strength and passion in the runner's faces as they push themselves beyond limits to finish just a step ahead of the person in front of them was incredible; like nothing else. If they ever made a movie about high school cross country, then this emotion would be almost impossible to match by an actor or actress. *This… is what it's all about.*

To the very last girl to cross over the finish line, every one of them fought their hardest to the end. It was only about two minutes between when the first and last girl crossed the finish line. In most regular season meets, this difference is five minutes or more.

No time was wasted, because the second the final girl hobbled down the finish chute, the starting line was filling up with guy teams. The crowd around the beginning of the course mashed together. It took me a second to figure out what was going on. I was dodging crazed fans trying to run me over as they pushed and shoved to get the best view. It was shoulder-to-shoulder packed like an NYC subway during rush hour. My height could not compete with many of them, so I learned to duck underneath and move low – almost in a crawl. It was a long, dark, and risky tunnel, rapidly shifting with legs and strollers, but it popped me out just by the course where, from my hands and knees, I could easily see the guys in starting positions. I shifted focus from the guys in the background to the fat man in the middle. He was already raising his hand slowly with a gun. The whistle was blaring in his mouth. I could see it, but couldn't hear a thing. Then the gun blasted, and it all happened way too fast. By the time the nerve impulse from my ears registered as information in my brain, and by the time that information was sent down to tell my legs to get up and run in the direction of everyone else… the runners had already breezed by me.

The crowd was already off in a massive mosaic of colors and commotion. Everyone had different ideas about the best place on the course to see the runners next, so they were all running off in different directions, and I tried to spot Central people and follow them. I thought I spotted a small group of blue, black, and white that must have been Central people about 30 meters in front of me. The majority of the crowd seemed to aimlessly follow one another and quickly migrate somewhere off to the left in the direction of the runners. My team members were going straight back towards a group of hills and trees a little to the right of everyone else.

I ran for a moment, trying my hardest to keep up with someone. The thicket of people began to dissipate. The noise and cheering roared off in the distance in a series of waves. I was spending too much effort on keeping up, not really knowing where I was going. I soon realized I was farther off than I had thought. The sound faded as I followed the small group of people who I thought were my teammates up to a lone group of trees on a hill. They were still a good 25 meters in front of me. I looked around to find where the cheers were drifting to. I turned back and realized the people I followed into the trees were gone. That was when I felt the silence of the atmosphere crash down on me.

It was a vertigo-ish experience. The trees surrounding me from all angles towered above, much bigger than they looked like from the outside. The faint cheers were coming from all around me, not from one direction anymore, but as if they were coming from the trees themselves. I couldn't decide what direction to go. The trees and brush were suddenly too thick, and I couldn't see anyone around. I could just hear them faintly, like I was standing in the middle of a large ballroom while ghosts waltzed around me.

It had only been about a minute since the gun went off. My spontaneous isolation happened fast. This is about how quickly one can lose themselves when watching a cross-country race. I let out a what-to-do-now sigh as I realized I was lost. I couldn't see traces of the crowd, but just hear them. I looked around with my hands on my hips, frustrated that nature was playing annoying games with me. I heard a louder cheer in the distance from behind me, a direction I apparently hadn't looked. I turned and noticed a small opening in the brush, the perfect size for a door. The trees bent in an arch over a trail leading out. It was like a constructed exit from the woods, crafted by the spirits in the trees. Under the mystical arch was a seemingly bald man sitting down, silhouetted by the sun outside the woods. He was watching the race. I walked up to the exit. As I walked closer, the person remained turned toward the outside with his profile to me. I started to recognize him as his definition materialized. He surely must of heard my feet crunching on the leaves.

"Ford? Is that you?" It is hard to explain, but somehow I already knew who it was. I could see the muscles, the shiny silver dog tag reflecting a glare, and the shaved head, and there was some aura that told me who he was. He wore camo-pants, and a white t-shirt with a brown leather fighter jacket. He didn't act surprised. He didn't even turn, but somehow he noticed me.

"They're in the middle, more towards the front in a tight group." He was informing me of the status of the Central guys in the race. *Perhaps a simple "hi" would have worked just as well.*

"Yeah... yeah great," I said. "Haven't seen you for a while." He finally glanced at me. He just nodded with a slight smile and turned back to the outside. I felt like he was inviting me to sit by him. I hesitated for a second, and went to meet him under the arch of branches. Surprisingly, he had an awesome sight of the race, like it was his secret spot. It was amazing. We were on a hill far away from everything, but we had a good bird's eye view of most all the course as it weaved in and out of trees and stretched around curves. We also had a pretty good shot of the finish line, which was in the corner of our view all the way to the right. I could see the long pack of runners going in the first group of trees in the course. In and out, in and out, they laced through the forest like thread through a grandma-knitted scarf. They stayed a long and connected group like a giant worm or creature from *Tremors* (1990, Kevin Bacon).

20 seconds must have passed while we sat there staring at the runners below. Then it hit me. *Wait a second... why the heck is this guy here? In Jefferson City for a cross-country meet – half the state away....* I started to utter something, but he interrupted.

"You wonder what they're thinking about..."

What!? He heard my thought. "There's got to be something worth talking about – something that's going on inside of their heads." I

180

loved the fact that whenever this guy talked to me, he would hardy ever issue the necessary establishing words in his sentences so that the rest of them made sense. He just assumed that other people were right with him when he was thinking. Or maybe he wasn't ever issuing conversation, just thinking aloud.

"Right," I said. "What do you think?"

"Hmm..." he started. I felt proud; for the first time I thought I had stumped him because I got him to say "hmm." "Whatever's worth it to them... I mean, I don't think anyone can worry about anything at that moment... it's got to be something spiritual - even if they don't realize it." He paused as we watched runners turn a sharp corner. "They're completely focused. There can only be one thing they're thinking," he added. I had to sit and think about this one. *Hmm...*

"I see. So, what are you doing all the way up here anyway? Do you have a brother or sister that runs or..." He didn't turn to me as he said "I graduate this May, and I'll go to basic in the fall. I was about to ask him where, but the long worm of runners began migrating toward us; merging from a group of trees about 300 meters away. Ford's keen eyes followed them intently.

"It's amazing right?" he said. *Gee, you can't go anywhere in a conversation with him.*

"Totally," I added, pretending to make sense of him. "It's sort of graceful and intense at the same time... but they're minds are all connected to something else other than the race." I kept my eyes on the runners. Hundreds of long strides; all in sync. It *was* sort of graceful, yet they all had faces showing this horrible pain and unblinking concentration at the same time. He seemed to give me a second to ingest his comments, and then turned toward me.

"That's it." He realized I didn't understand. "That's why I'm here... He turned back. "Why wouldn't people want to come to their school teams state championships? And I'm visiting family in Jeff City." I looked down at the front-runners. Their legs glided like deer across the fields, moving as smooth as Santa's reindeer in the clouds.

"So how are you feeling Johnny?" "Oh good, good." Silence... *Umm...* "Great... yeah."

"So is the cancer all gone, or are you still taking a small dose of chemo or...?" It was only about the thousandth time I'd been asked that one.

"Oh yeah. Completely done. It's all gone. All I can do now is recover and... just pray it never comes back."

"That makes two of us..." he answered me quickly, as if he had been waiting to say it. "I think you're an amazing guy. I really respect guys like you." *Guys like me?* I didn't know quite how to respond to that one.

"Gee thanks man, it sure means a lot."

Central was in the middle of the long worm of runners who all disappeared behind some rolling hills. "So what kind of stuff do you do?" I asked Ford. Despite the race that was almost ten minutes in, I strangely felt a tad more comfortable talking to him, and there was an odd pull at my conscience to find out more, so I decided to keep the conversation going.

"So I graduate in May," he said. "As I mentioned, I'm going to join the Army." *Has his priorities set...*

"That's awesome man." He sounded proud of this last statement. "Really, I think that is one of the coolest things... people joining the army. So, that's what you really want to do?" He had turned back to the race with a sort of dramatic intensity. He answered quickly and confidently, like the response was second nature.

"I'm supposed to." (Another strange answer I wasn't sure how to respond to.)

"Aw... I see. So are your parents making you or something?" I asked.

"No, it's just my purpose. I know it is - I'm supposed to." He turned to me again; he now had a more serious look on his face, not sternness, but like he was about to unload deep thoughts. "Ever since I was a kid Johnny... I've loved the army, everything it stands for; the thrill, the honor. But there's a reason I love it. I go outside myself and look at me... I look at myself, and about what I love... It's my God given purpose." He paused for almost too long while I just stared at him. "Why do you run?"

Our short conversation was going too deep too fast. This guy's predilection to speak in Jesus-like mind-penetrating parables had gotten the best of me. I understood what he was talking about, but my comfort level of discussing purpose and love with someone I didn't know all too well was short. The worm of runners was coming around a hill back towards us now. They were heading around our hideout of trees and were going to pass very close to us in about ten seconds. It was like a locomotive approaching from far away; the ground starts to shake with intensity and the rumble only grows louder until it screams past you, knocking you aside with the power. It was the perfect excuse to cut off the conversation with Ford. I didn't even respond to his last question.

"Woa, they're coming this way!" I said excitedly. Ford stood up with me to watch. The runners must have overheard our conversation, and demanding our full attention, they telepathically averted our ears to the sound of the stampede. If they did, they weren't being selfish, because they deserved it. Ford must of have imagined it being their "purpose."

I dashed to the course, which came around close to the bundle of trees. The first runner was some 50 meters away and the giant wiggly worm stretched behind him for about 300 meters. I looked back to see if Ford Swoon was behind me, but he was gone, having vanished in a matter of seconds like an apparition. He must have either been following the runners, or he hid himself back in the trees, plotting his next psychological tactic to mess with someone else's mind.

The first runner zoomed past me like one of those show-off motorcyclist that make too much noise, leaving a trail of wind that rustled the thin hair on my head that had started to grow back. It was baby hair, like that of a one-year-old: fine, soft, and swift to be blown about by the slightest breeze. He was about 20 meters ahead of everyone else. I didn't catch his team name. But his uniform was purple and yellow, *One of those pesky Kansas City schools.* I didn't notice any letters on the side of his jersey that might have been for another teammate of his missing in action, like JHP. The next 30 or so runners came by at the same speed. Then I saw my team. They were doing great. They had stuck together, running in a tight pack the whole way. There is something about running next to your teammate. You push each other, and everyone runs faster and more efficiently. I yelled as they passed. Most of them were so focused they didn't notice me. Peter Fontane glanced up though, and nodded. His muscles strained and his face was tired, but he kept a perfect running form. Johnny Rivera looked up as well. He was struggling a little more than Peter, but he forced a smirk as he slapped his hand over the JHP strip sewn on his shoulder and winked.

The time was almost 12 minutes, which meant the end was near. State runners would start finishing anywhere between 14 and 17 minutes. I waited for the last runner to pass before I started going as fast as I could to the finish line. I didn't get to watch much of the race, so I wanted to be sure and get a good spot by the finish chute. As I ran, I kept looking back for Ford. *So he came here by himself just to watch these races… Cause he loves to watch people run… because they're… graceful?* I thought hard as I came down to the finish chute, wheezing like I had just run a whole race. Coach O'Brien and Coach Price were down there hopping up and down and flailing their arms by the chute. Just behind the hill was the giant wiggly worm advancing powerfully, puffing steam from their faces. The crowd around the chute was funneling in fast and the roar grew quickly. I secured a spot about ten feet away from the chute, holding on tight to the ropes so that crazed fans wouldn't run me over.

The motorcycle like guy was still in front. The crowd was hanging so far over the ropes that everyone could smell the body odor through the wind as he whizzed by, especially me with my radiated extra-sensitive nose. A mass of runners was close behind him. *Second! Third!.. Fourth – Fifth – Sixth!* Amazing! - the guys were fighting for their lives as they came in, fighting so hard to outrun the opponent breathing down their neck, shoulders battling it out in a road rage. *Seventh! Eighth! Ninth! Tenth!* All in a just couple of seconds time. *Whoa! Whoa! Whoa!* I could no longer keep count. It was like when you try to count the number of cars on a passing train. You start going, the counting gets faster and faster, but you just can't keep up, and lose it. It seemed like about 30 guys passed the finish line before I saw the Central group. They were still running in a tight pack as I saw before. They looked good, still running strong. It was only in the last 200 meters that they broke apart into all-out sprints. All seven of them crossed the finish line within seconds.

I was screaming so loud. "Blaaaaahhhh!!!!!! Yeeeahhhhh!!!! Bleeeeeaah!" I'm not sure what I was screaming, but I wanted them to know I was there. It was just a screechy wail of nonsense among the hundreds, but I wanted them to hear it, and even though they couldn't physically, they did in their heads, and most likely in their left shoulders.

16
Back in St. Joe

December, 2000

The lively social atmosphere, the warm smell of reliable wholesome food with that tinge of honey barbecue sauce and the reasonable prices were just right for a small band of high school kids on a night out. The neighborhood *Applebees* was the place to go.

"So how'd you guys do at State?" Cory asked. Six of us were sitting on bar stools at one of those tall circular tables. "The guys finished fourth… we did really good."

"That-a-boy Johnny!" Cory slapped me on the back. He knew I didn't run at State, but still thought of me as part of the team. The guys finished in 16, 17, 18, 20, 21, 22, and 24th place - an amazing finish that won them 3rd place overall.

By that time, my hair had grown to look almost normal from the front. It was still thin, and there was no hair in the very back surrounding the surgery site. Therefore, I kept it all pretty short so that it would appear somewhat even. It sort of looked like I meant to shave it bald in the back, but it exposed the long red scar down the deformed lower right side of my head and neck.

"How did *you* guys do at State?" Cory played varsity soccer. All of us knew the soccer team did not make it to State; they didn't even make it past Sectionals. The cross-country team was the best sport at Central, better in the sense that the team won most every meet and frequently competed at State. The soccer team was probably the second best in that respect, but nobody came to watch cross-country meets; no one ever talked about it, but everyone went to the soccer games. So it was a trade-off I guess. It was Cory, Gilleland, Twombly, Norty, Jackson, and I at that round table in the Applebee's - at the mid-point of our high school years. I loved those moments. It was moments like that when I felt completely normal. The only thing that wasn't normal about going out were the little kids that would come in with their parents. We were sitting across from some couple and a little kid and his brother or something in a booth. My right side was facing them, and they wouldn't quit staring at me and the mysterious havoc on the back of my head. It was like they thought the back of my head held the answers to all of their fourth grade tests. This kind of thing happened all of the time whenever I went out, and frequently still does. I tried my hardest not to notice or think about it in any way, but the truth is, I struggled every time not to strangle the many ignorant young onlookers.

After sitting for a while with our empty water glasses, the waiter finally approached us. He spoke up in a friendly "I better get a good tip from you bastards" sort of tone. "Hey guys, are you all ready to order?" Cory ordered his lime chicken.

"I'll have the strip steak medium rare please," I said to the zit-faced waiter with the pubescent voice. I assumed I was done so I folded up my menu and set it at the end of the table. I turned my attention away from him as he started to take the other orders. Silence...

"Sir?" Silence...

"Cathcart!" Gilleland said. *Whoa... Oh gee, he's still talking to me.* The waiter was mumbling something. I assumed he asked me if that was all I wanted. "Right," I assured the waiter.

"Um..." he said, and repeated his mumble. Only this time I understood it because I was looking at his face as he asked me a little louder, "What would you like for your vegetable? A twice-baked potato, mashed or fries?" A warm wave of embarrassment flushed my face.

"Oh, I'm sorry." *Crap, what's wrong with me...* "Mashed, please." "Alrighty," the waiter squeaked. Then he started to take the other orders. I made sure this time by watching his lips and listening intently that he wasn't talking to me anymore. Then I decided it was OK to let go.

Cory smiled at me while shaking his head downward and giggling. This has happened to me several times before. I'll say the wrong things in a conversation because I didn't hear things right or at all. The guys knew I had a problem, and they understood. They were my best friends in the world and nothing was personal. So we always made fun of each other when we did stupid things.

"He'll have a Coke," Gilleland said to the waiter, referring to me. They all started chuckling. I looked up at the waiter. "Um… What would you like to drink sir?" *What? I did it again? I'm an idiot!* "I'll just have water." I said.

I knew my hearing was damaged. I knew what was going on, but all my doctors had told me that, although not ever back to normal, my hearing would get slightly better once the remains of chemo completely left my body. And they said it would be close to a year before that happened, so I had faith that my hearing wouldn't be so bad for so long.

Some people told me some of the tissue may get better, but ear cells are neurological cells. Just like brain cells, they don't regenerate like every other cell in your body. The ones you are born with are the only ones you have, and if you lose them, they are gone.

• • •

June 2001

It was the middle of the hot, muggy months of summer break after junior year. During the summer, the cross-country team meets every other morning to train for the upcoming season. They aren't regular practices for the team, but there is a group within my church called Wyatt Park Runner's Club, and the team members are part of that during summers.

I had been jogging more and more on my own, and by the end of the school year, I felt I could keep up with someone. I decided to run with Wyatt Park Runner's Club that summer. I drove a black

Chevy Blazer my parents bought me when I turned 16 earlier that year. They had the license plate personalized: RUN JHP. Every detail of this moment is forever ingrained in my head. I was driving up that long, gravel drive in my trademark car to the spot at the college, the same area we met for real practices. Everyone was already there, stretching in a group as usual. Their heads looked over when they saw my Blazer rolling up the drive. The cloud of debris following me must have dramatized it like in one of those truck commercials. As I got out of the car and walked up to meet my group of supporting athletes, one girl started clapping. Then everyone else joined in and did a standing ovation. Tears would have slipped down my face, as they do when I write this, but at that moment, their applause only gave me a strength, a joy, and an incredible sense of immortal confidence that I was officially back in the game.

I trained with the runner's club all summer long. I worked out every day at the YMCA with my friend Jackson. He spotted me on all of the lifts until I regained strength to do them on my own. In time, my muscles toned, and my endurance grew.

• • •

"John…" Dad said with a concerned voice. It was also a stern one, but not stern like I'd done something wrong - but stern like he was about to give me the sex talk. Dad, Mom and I sat around the dinner table at our new house. They both tried to look at me seriously, but it seemed they couldn't. I humored myself with watching the two trade turns attempting to talk. There was some sort of impenetrable wall between whatever they were about to tell and their tongues.

"John… how are you hearing at school?" *They know the answer…* "Um… well, yah know… ok."

"John, have you ever thought about… ways of possibly… making your hearing better; maybe taking advantage of the technology these days." *I know very well what they're talking about…*

189

"What are you guys talking about?" They glanced at each other as if they were going to play rock paper scissors to see who got to say the next two words. "Hearing aids John. We think…" I abruptly interjected. "Noooooooo way. There is no way I'm ever going to wear hearing aids… No."

"Honey?" they reacted in surprised question, as if they really weren't expecting me to solemnly object. "John, they would really help you." Mom said.

"What? No, my ears aren't going to grow. Besides, that wouldn't have anything to do with it. I can get along without them," I said.

"See John?" "What?" "You can't understand a word we're saying." Dad was getting aggravated. I obviously must have heard something wrong.

"John," Mom added, thinking it would change my mind, "You know, they have those really tiny ones that nobody can see." This did appeal to me a little. I knew I needed something, I wanted to hear, but I couldn't stand the thought of it. *I would be labeled as the hearing aid person… the kid with problems.* I could hear everyone's thoughts like a parade through my head. They were marching in circles around my broken skull, blowing horns and chanting, *"Oohh… be nice to him, but be careful because he's fragile, he can't hear." "Don't date him because he's sick, he might hurl on you, but make sure you're nice to him." "That guy right there… when you talk to him, make sure you say everything loud and clear and maybe repeat it… just like you're talking to your grandpa."*

I started feeling sick. I almost did hurl on the layers of warm red lasagna spread out all over my plate. A flush of nausea and a stream of tears ran down my face. I stormed off to go find Mr. Mischief.

17
24/7

September, 2001

Some nights, when I'm up late studying or writing a paper, I get
these cravings... cravings for cereal. There's something about a
craving that unleashes a beast within that won't stop until
complete satisfaction. The crunchy morsels of baked corn and rice
stained with attractive commercial colors and loaded with refined
sugar that disguises itself in multiple different flavors such as
fruit, baked goods, cookies, or even a filet mignon. This mind-
mesmerizing taste is an experience. The cold splash of creamy
whole milk filtered through the seductive cereals is something I
must have.

I was a junior now. It was the second month into school and one
night I was up late trying to concentrate on an a paper for
English class.

It was so hard though, when all I could think about was the filling
sensation of cold crunchy cereal and milk cascading down my dry
throat in a refreshing waterfall of beauty. I got up from my
computer, and walked down the hall to the kitchen. The feeling
was getting closer as I approached the point where I could hear
the hum of the refrigerator. I turned the corner and there it was,
staring at me, screaming at me. I popped open the cupboard and
almost couldn't handle the smile growing on my face when I
pulled out the box of Fruit Loops. I grabbed one of my favorite
bowls, a white ceramic one with a blue ring around the top edge.
Cereal tastes best out of a ceramic bowl, just as Coke tastes best
from a glass bottle. Once the clattering sound of the cereal hitting
the surface of the bowl tickled my ears, I turned back to the
fridge, the legendary gate guarding the heavenly milk. I
approached it like Indiana Jones approached the series of possible
Holy Grails. I carefully opened the gate, and the cold air hit me all

at once with a slap. The shelves revealed a beautiful, shimmering – empty bottle of whole milk.

The pangs of rage and sorrow flew up my brains and arms so fast, like the transformation of Dr. Jekyll to Mr. Hyde. I couldn't quite handle the intense remorse, and I almost fell to my knees, quivering under my milkless reality. It took me a second to shake off the drama and regain control of myself. I turned to the clock with only one option in mind. It was 2:30 in the morning, later than I had expected. My paper was due in five and a half hours. But as I said, cravings bring out the beast in a person. I was still in pajamas, but I stepped into some black dress shoes that were nearest in sight, threw on a brown leather bomber coat Dad used to wear, grabbed my keys and headed out the door to the Wal-Mart.

One of the great things about living at our new house, was that the Wal-Mart was just down the road. It only took a minute or two to get there, and it was open 24/7. So whenever drastic situations like that arose, all hope was not lost, for I could always count on Wal-Mart.

Wal-Mart is a simply delightful place to go at night. If you go during the day, you are liable to get trampled - not just by overweight soccer moms spending hours in every aisle eyeing the shelves for the best low-fat "Great Values," or by people too large to walk themselves and carelessly racing handicapped scooters around like the 101 – but also by everyone in town marching up and down the crowded aisles, eternally searching for the glorious Mr. Rollback.

This is why I enjoy being there during the late hours, not just at night, but in the morning; at 2:00 or 3:00. At 4:00, you might encounter the more elite group of senior citizens who jog the aisles. At those times, don't be foolish and get caught with cholesterol-reducing cheerios, or you will be tackled.

The person at the entrance smiled at me. I think it's their full-time job, smiling at people, and nodding. I liked that. I knew right where to go, to the very back wall where the milk is stored behind the glass doors. Like orphans, they all wait quietly in their cold positions for owners to take them away. I grabbed one and I started walking back to the front of the store, keeping a sharp eye for cruising seniors, or nocturnal undead warriors. I passed each aisle with increasing speed. " Wheo, Wheo, Wheo!" I don't really know why, but I was never in a hurry to come, yet always in a hurry to leave.

Just as I sped past the cereal aisle, I plunged into someone backing their way out and I got a mouthful of arm! The split second I was in contact with the arm, my nose involuntarily took a whiff. I looked up. The blue Wal-Mart vest was typical; "How can I help you?" *Mr. Rollback...* There was a shaved head and camouflage shirt underneath the vest. This is totally the truth. It was Ford Swoon.

"Whoa… hey man. Pardon me – totally. I run into you in the most random places. You work here?" Unshaken from the crash, he began unloading a tall lopsided stack of cereal boxes from a dolly onto a shelf. He didn't even act surprised to bump into me.

"Yeah, it's good money." He didn't say anything else. He just kept unloading and glanced at me like he was waiting for me to say something.

"You graduated last year, I thought you would be off at basic or something?" I asked. I don't think he heard what he was expecting, what he necessarily wanted to hear, or if he just didn't hear me at all.

"If all of the employees at Wal-Mart were clerks, then who would unload the trucks and restock the shelves?" he asked me. *Here we go...* My eyes left him every so often to follow the beautiful cereal boxes as he stood them up on the shelves. "If the whole staff were comprised of auto mechanics, then who would greet people at the door?"

"Um…" I wasn't surprised by his sudden tangent. In fact, I was not expecting a normal response from him at all. I had run into Ford Swoon enough to know that, and here he is working the night shift at Wal-mart. I recognized the metaphor behind his statement, so I decided to counteract with a likewise philosophical claim of my own. "If the foot should say 'Since I am not a hand, then I do not belong to the body, would it not for that reason cease to be part of the body?" I believe my morph to his pun-like level worked, like I broke a code, or spoke the password. He knew right where I was. He looked at me and half smiled.

"1st Corinthians 12," he said. I smiled back. He finally started to respond to my first question. "I don't really work here anymore. Basic is over. In a few weeks, they're shipping me off – somewhere overseas. There's a lot of things about to happen you know, in light of what's been going on." *He's talking about 9/11.*

"Are you ready?" I asked. He focused his eyes at me a second time and smiled like he was about to tell me an inside joke, "Ready or not… here I come," he said. *My goodness! This guy's a total frickin nerd…*

"Like I said last year, it's what I love. He has shaped my heart to fulfill his purpose… through me." He talked like he was 100% certain this was true. I could tell he was talking about God. "We've all got things to do Johnny. I unload trucks, and I fight. In these, I glorify God." His words were dipping to levels far too deep for me again. I didn't want to bring it deeper. "Well sure," I said. "Thanks…. For the um, wisdom, yah know." His face did grow a little stern. My eyes left him for the cereal. As he pulled off boxes from the top, his stack became more and more unstable. There was one box that was close to falling. It inched closer and closer to the edge with every one of Ford's movements - a glimmering box of Corn Pops.

"They say it's about what you do with what you have…" His eyes stayed on me, jumping from my right eye to my left; checking to see if his crazy words had registered in either, or rather which one he would deliver his final ones to. "…But what are you really doing? What's in it? What drives it? It's also important what you have in what you do; if that makes sense."

I wasn't surprised that it made no sense. I don't believe I ever asked for Ford Swoon's philosophical reasoning about purpose in life, but the fact that he was as dorky as he was – made me feel sorry for him, and I wanted to listen. I wanted to understand fully what he was saying. It is bizarre that there are people like this in the world who are engaging to this level, but lacking in other aspects. I believe, in a roundabout way, to have a voice or a metaphor people want to listen to, or want to understand, you have to be a little bit, or completely off-the-wall like Ford Swoon.

This guy had irritated and baffled me in the past, but, awkwardly, at that moment, I was starting to a develop a respect for him.

The box of Corn Pops finally leaped out from the side of the stack, plunging toward the floor. It seemed to fall into my right hand which quickly grabbed it before it crashed to the ground. Ford quickly glanced at me, impressed by my reflexes. This was a good point to leave, so I started to walk away.

"You take care of yourself." I said that, and I think I heard him say, "Yes sir." He saluted me. Glad to be leaving, I saluted him back with the box of Corn Pops.

. . .

I kept telling myself that no one would notice, no one would care, no one would say anything. *It's just like wearing glasses.* My game plan was simple: to act completely normal like nothing was different. "John, nobody will think twice about it."

"John, you have such a cute face that people won't notice." My parents thought that presenting me with these various guarantees would alleviate my self-consciousness about wearing hearing aids. Hearing aids in high school - I was sure the stunt would set me far back in the race to becoming normal. It took a long battle between my parents, Gajjar, and myself, to finally agree that I was going to get some. The one phrase that made me give in was actually from my grandma.

"Well you know John, a hearing loss is much more noticeable than a hearing aid."

OK, well, at least we can get those ones they advertise on TV, the invisible ones. That's a big hoax. Those little tiny hearing aids don't do crap. There is no room for power, no room for comfort, and a definite quantity/quality issue. Plus, those hearing aids don't fit in my ear canal. They only fit in old people's ear canals that are big and expanded with age. As much as I hated it, we had to go with the behind-the-ear hearing aids. BTE hearing aids are large locust-shaped gadgets that rest behind each ear. In these - as opposed to the invisible "completely-in-the-canal" hearing aids, the larger and more obvious "in-the-canal" ones, and the fat blobs "in-the-ear" - there is room for a whole digital computer, two directional microphones that can focus on certain sounds in front or behind you, a button where you can adjust up to four different audio channels, and a volume adjuster. These babies were also top-of-the-line powerful. The thing is though, that they were absolutely huge. They were each about an inch and a half long and about half an inch wide. They rest behind the ear so if I had hair, it would help cover them up, but I only had a little bit of thin hair, definitely not enough to spare in order to help cover up the massive devices.

• • •

I entered through the door leading into the JROTC quarters. It's on the opposite side of the building from Coach O'Brien's room and well away from the main entrance to the high school. There is a thin flight of steps that drops you into one of the hallways. Few people use this entrance, and it was a good entrance to use if you had something to hide. It was ridiculous... trying to hide it, trying to avoid people. No one can hide a beet juice stain on a white shirt. People were going to see, and there was nothing I could do about it.

As I walked into the hallway, the heavy commotion was normal. Folks were all around hanging out by lockers flirting, studying, or shoving books in and out. A group of four JROTC guys and one girl walked down the hallway, heading toward me and the stairs leading down to the JROTC headquarters. I didn't know two of the guys, but I could tell they were JROTC because of the shaved heads, the dog tags, and the brownish green color scheme in their outfits. I had seen the girl before; I knew she was JROCT because of her mullet, and her obsession with wearing combat boots. The other guy was Jerry. I had not seen him all summer, and he looked grown up, with a more muscular build and a look of maturity deep in his expression. As they approached, he nodded at me and his straight mouth broke into a smile.

"Hey Johnny, how are you?" "Excellent man," I said. "You're lookin' good." "Yeah yeah, well, good to see you Johnny. Are you feeling good?"

He hasn't forgotten. "I'm feeling great. Thanks. Well I'll see ya later man."

"Alright, see ya Johnny." He totally walked up to me, shook my hand, and walked off. He didn't notice anything. Well, I'm sure he did, but didn't say anything.

"Hey Johnny, what's up?" This sophomore I knew came up suddenly behind me. "Hey, what's that on your ear Johnny?" *Bingo!*

"Headphones, that tell me to breathe in and out."

"Hmmm… looks like some sort of hearing aid to me. Are you having trouble hearing Johnny?"

Throughout the day I saw most people who I would expect to say something about my hearing aids, and a lot of them did. Many of them didn't, but I saw them look directly at them and struggle not to say anything as if it were a mole on my nose. I almost felt better when people asked me about them, just so I could set it straight with them. As nice and respectable as everyone tried to

197

be, my old-people hearing aids stuck out for everyone to see and cast an unbearable weight not only on my ears, but to my weakening self-confidence. They were uncomfortable, ugly, and what's worse, they made everything sound like it was coming from a computer. Every voice was electronically generated like that robot voice in the Beastie Boys song *Intergalactic*.

High school pop culture can have a wrath that attacks those weak-minded individuals who ever feel sorry for themselves, and only drives them deeper into a feeling of isolation. However, I refused to consider myself a weak-minded individual. The large impenetrable wall of mainstream high school society is supported by a conspiracy – one which strives to make anyone who is the slightest bit different from everyone else feel awkwardly unwelcome. I was only different because I had cancer. I felt so wronged, so violated, so abused.

· · ·

I had trained like a boxer over the summer - running three to six miles a day, frequently lifting weights, sprinting the football stadium bleachers while punching at the air and listening to *Eye of the Tiger*. I did all of this with the mindset that I was avenging myself. I finished with a perfect training summer. Senior year had just begun, and I was ready for the final cross-country season.

I entered the crazed locker room with more confidence each day. I started arriving earlier, and I even got better dibs on the toilet because I was an upperclassmen. I stepped up to one of the broken mirrors in the old locker room and smirked at the results of my hard work, gazing at the almost normal teenager that I was becoming. My muscles were defined and my hair had grown back more. The spitting image of a competitive runner with decent hair looked back at me in the mirror. I still hated my hearing aids, but I had gotten used to wearing them like they were glasses. The mechanical sound molded to my brain so that it was normal now. I just always tried not to think about people looking at them from behind, questioning their presence with the giant red scar in the back. I still had the urge to ring the necks of little kids who stared at my head, but I had learned to always take a deep breath, count five sheep, and let it go.

Running had soon become the addiction that it once was, and I was constantly getting better at it. At practices over the summer, I was running as one of the top Junior Varsity athletes. Once the season had started back up, I finished better and better at races, shaving off my PR (personal record) times with every meet.

I was heavily involved in my church. I actually went for a reason now – a reason I understood. I was going because I wanted to go – because I knew and experienced the God and the Holy Spirit that I went for, not because I was otherwise doomed to hell.

Little by little, things started to get beautiful again. I was sure now, that life *was* a gift from God. I already looked back at what I went through like it was a thing of the past never to bother me again. Despite the side effects, I still had a totally able body. I had friends, I was an athlete, and I knew I had an incredible story to share with people for as long as I live.

It sure looked like things were getting back to normal. I had a few scars, but I learned to deal with them, and I think they only made me stronger.

18
Denny's and Mrs. Swoon

October, 2002

One of my favorite things to do is to go out to places late at night - really late at night. There's a certain peace about it. It's sort of like an idiosyncratic connection with the stillness. Everyone is home asleep, no one is out, the streets are empty and dark, but it's not an empty feeling… not at all. You are alone with the stars. The spirits seem to be out at night.

It was about 1:00 A.M. I was supposed to meet Jerry at the Denny's in 15 minutes. We had run into each other at school more and more over the past year, and I started to enjoy his nerd-like presence. We even started to hang out sometimes outside of school. We had planned on the Denny's that night.

Usually, I don't go hang out with Jerry's kind of people; they are not my usual close friends. However, I have learned, by socializing with his type every once in a while, you can learn a lot. By his type, I mean someone different from your usual close friends, someone who might not think the same as you.

I love how when you go out in St. Joe in the middle of a weeknight, it will seem like a ghost town, but there are always cars filling up the lot at the only 24/7 restaurant. In the middle of all the darkness, the Denny's always has its lights on. Inside, you'll find the stereotypical late-nighters hanging around in the grease-coated booths, flirting with exhausted waitresses in stained aprons parading coffee and pancakes around like slaves. Here you'll find the majority of the mullet population sitting around with their elbows on the table criticizing, in ridiculously loud voices, their hometown meteorologist, or a small group of baggy-panted high school kids, smoking and ranting tasteless jokes about their hot girlfriends, or the random stressed loner who's just had a hard day and needs a late night pancake. Then there are weirdos like Jerry and I who occasionally get together, drink coffee, and talk about life.

"Johnny..." Our waitress walked up to us with two coffee mugs and poured them full. The steam rose up in waves like a dancing cobra. Jerry took a sip.

"If you want, Johnny, you're welcome to come along..." Jerry said. Jerry's head was shaved; he no longer had shaggy, dirty hair. This brought out more of his nerdy look, but made him appear wiser at the same time. Jerry was asking me about joining a writing club he belonged to, and about coming to a meeting where they get drunk off pop and discuss each other's work. I was surprised to hear Jerry tell me about his interest in an art. *Writing? Wow, I've been completely wrong about this guy all along.*

"Writing?"

"Yeah, we write short stories and poetry on our own and get together to talk about them... and there's free pop."

"So... what kind of writing do you guys do? Like fantasy, wizards and dragons?" Our waitress walked over and poured our mugs full again.

"Yeah! Sometimes. Mostly it's just creative stuff, yah know, stuff people write poetry about, I don't know.... Like me, I'll often come up with poetry or a short story based off of an experience... or a person I've met. If I'm going to do something like write about dragons, then I'll make those dragons be like people I've met and don't like."

Jerry was an interesting character. I had never heard of a high school kid that wore camo to school every day, large glasses and combat boots that didn't fit, and got off on writing short stories. The awkwardness of our in-depth conversation only kept me interested in it. I was fascinated with the cleverness behind his flow of words, and recognized his love for whatever he did.

"Man… that's pretty interesting, that you like to do that. I don't know if I'd have such an awesome time at your club, but thanks for the invite, yah know." He took a sip of coffee as I kept talking.

"I don't think I could do that. I mean, all of those rules about writing in school, it totally turned me off. I just got burnt out with writing… that's all." His eyebrows lowered a little as he listened. He still had a slight smile in his face like he was proud to talk about the subject, and proud to tell me what he was about to tell me.

"Well, Johnny… It's not really like that. There is a lot that goes into writing a story or any kind of writing more than what… everyone teaches in school." He kept pausing. He was thinking carefully about his words. "It seems that a lot of people get the wrong message if they think too much about storytelling. It's not about rules, or going through motions they teach in class. Writing poetry isn't about guidelines you have to worry about following in order for it to be "correct" for other people. He did little quotation signs with his fingers. "That's not really the purpose. It's more about this… connection, joy I guess… for being creative through words, and just seeing what other people come up with." He paused after this statement. "It's just… Hmmm. You should come to the meeting and just try it out. It's something that you really just have to experience for yourself."

I enjoyed talking with Jerry. I liked how he had a strong passion for his hobby. What he was saying did make sense to me, and it made me think. I tried to take another sip, but I realized my coffee had become a tiny lukewarm puddle. Jerry started to say something else, but was cut off by a man who seemed to appear at our table. He was a nice-looking, young adult around six feet tall with nicely combed short brown hair. He wore a white polo and blue jeans. He had a generally kind look about him. The man knelt beside us on his right knee and introduced himself.

"Hey guys, my name is Daniel. I'm from Westhill Baptist Church. How you doin' fellas?" I immediately thought of my experience at Westhill, and the man that "saved" me. I quickly determined that this was not the same person, for he had a small, smooth chin, and he was younger, possibly 25. First of all, I didn't feel comfortable being referred to by a complete stranger named Daniel as a "fella," It's just like I hate when you walk into one of those teeny bopper stores and two or three workers come up to you and say, "Hey bro…" or "Hey buddy, can I help you?" *You don't know me, don't call me buddy. Don't call me fella.* But it was his next words that really made me feel weird.

"Are you Johnny Cathcart?"

"Um…" I didn't know what to say. I must have nodded or something, because he went on.

"I thought I recognized you." He paused and held his smile. "Johnny, I know about what you've been through. You've been on our prayer list at Westhill for quite some time now. I saw you sitting down, and just wanted to come let you know that I think you're awesome for what you've done." He turned to Jerry.

"Hi, I'm Jerry." I could tell Jerry already didn't like this guy.

"Hi Jerry, I'm Daniel." Daniel reached out his hand to shake Jerry's. Then he didn't say anything for almost three seconds. He just smiled. It was incredibly awkward. Jerry and I were speechless, and both our mugs were empty. "So do you guys go to a church around here?" He asked this like he was accusing us of not going to a church. Jerry and I exchanged glances, and he slightly smirked at me.

Suddenly, we saw a woman approaching us from the other side of the restaurant. We were relieved because she was going break up the uncomfortable conversation with Daniel.

"Mrs. Swoon!" Jerry said, "What are you doing here?" *He knows this strange woman…* She was a little overweight, like she has come here often. I bet she was about 45, but the wrinkles and obvious stress in her face made her look much older. Her hair was shorter, and it was brown, but there were hints of gray. A few seconds passed and she did not say anything, but she had clearly stopped Daniel from talking. The lady was sniffling. Jerry spoke up again. "What's going on Joyce? Is everything all right?" *Mrs. Swoon…*

Mrs. Swoon... I made the connection; Jerry was friends with Ford, so this must be Ford's mother. Before she spoke, she actually turned to me. She composed her words between sniffles, like when you're trying to make a crying person feel better and you can't understand them because they are sniffling too much.

"You must be Johnny Cathcart." She said. *She knows who I am too.*

"Joyce, what's wrong?" Jerry said. Mrs. Swoon, or Joyce, sighed a sigh of sorrow, or maybe pity and turned back to him. "Oh…" She paused for a second.

"Jerry - how are you?" Jerry only responded with a concerned face, just like all JROTC people do when they sense there is trouble.

"Well," Mrs. Swoon started. I looked up at Daniel, wondering about his reaction. He was still on his knee, but had leaned back out of the way. His mouth was open a crack in astonishment. Mrs. Swoon continued. I glanced at Jerry and he performed a dry gulp, like he suddenly knew what was wrong. Jerry scooted over and Joyce sat down at our booth. "An officer came to my house the other day…" She paused to sniffle. A tear ran down a crease in her cheek. "…Ford is not alive anymore Jerry."

I saw Daniel's mouth grow open a little. *What in the world? How…* It just didn't seem to make any sense, what she just said. *Why would…* Jerry's face was now slowly moving down and his eyes settled upon the empty coffee mug. His face was sad, but he also had that look of a man who is tough on the inside and good at keeping his emotions at bay. Mrs. Swoon put her arms slightly around Jerry, "I'm so sorry honey… I'm so sorry." He took up her arms. "There was a mission happening, Operation Anaconda…" Every word from her mouth was diluted by tears and more sniffles. "It was just a few days ago in Afghanistan." *Afghanistan… Oh my gosh… Ford told me he was going to the army - the war…* I looked at Jerry and Mrs. Swoon. It now made sense to me why this lady was here at the Denny's alone so late at night. She had come here to sulk and eat pancakes.

Daniel was still near us. He had stood up now. He was scratching his head, probably thinking what he was to do, or how he was supposed to save us from the sting of tragic news. I wasn't too sad from the news that Ford Swoon was dead. I didn't know him very well, and I hadn't seen him for more than a year. I sniffled because of Jerry and Mrs. Swoon. It was hard to imagine what they were feeling at that moment. *Wait, she knew who I was?* She seemed to respond to my thoughts, just as Ford once did. Still embracing Jerry, she turned her head at me and sniffled.

"Johnny, Ford told me about you. He admired your courage, bravely fighting through everything you went through. You don't know this, but he was at the hospital during entire first surgery."

I didn't really know how to respond, and I just nodded. The situation was just too weird for me, too sudden. I almost felt like it was set up, like a staged act of drama trying to transmit a message, or implant some knowledge within me... perhaps a conspiracy between Jerry, Ford, his mother, and even Daniel. All of the characters were just too much to be real people. But staged or not, the emotion swarmed in me, tingling and rushing like the white goop right before my surgeries. "He told me so much about you Johnny. You were an inspiration to him - you and Jerry both." She smiled at me, a very big smile, but her face was still wet with heartbreak and pain. Mrs. Swoon then glanced at the strange man standing beside our table. Daniel finally found the perfect chance to say something.

"Ma'am, my name is Daniel. I was just chatting with the boys here. I'm so terribly sorry about your loss." He put his hand on her back lightly. "Ma'am... say, do you know Jesus?"

• • •

That night I was having trouble falling asleep. Some say that a walk on the beach at night, on a mountain top, or some sort of solitude with a starry night are good times to think and reflect upon the deeper meaning of things, like life. Some say that the best way to deal with your anger is to either punch at a pillow, punch at people, punch at walls, or exert any form of physical force on something less than you. The best time for me to do this is during a run. A run in the middle of the night when the gentle breeze and the silent air calms me, it sort of massages my thoughts.

When I say "running," I mean distance running. Simply running is not the same as distance running - not even close. A real distance run involves more than legs. It's almost like an extensive prayer, a prolonged meditation, a stretched moment of correlation between the most tranquil, stress-free elements of your spirit and and your muscles.

When on a distance run, the secure rhythm of my shoes battering down upon the earth pulls my mind beyond my head.

It made sense what happened, *people go to war and they die... reasonable...* Ford had such a strange impact on me that I still didn't understand. It was like there was something I had yet to do about it. It seemed like if I didn't think anything further of him, then he would become a ghost vanished from the world with unfinished business.

The air was cold, but crisp and refreshing. The second I stepped off my porch, I began running. The stars were scattered out all over the dark blue sky, lighting my path. The only sound audible was the rhythm of my feet hitting the pavement in the same natural key as my breathing... as well as the ringing in my ears, if you count that as a sound. The rest was the ambient nature of night silently singing its lullaby. Trees were like noble statues, simply acknowledging me as I passed. My long driveway turned into a village drive, and the village drive turned into road.

Ford's faint voice seemed to echo in my head. *"I'm going to join the Army... It's just my purpose."* His voice faded with the steady beat of my running. The totally trite phrase sounded almost silly. Once again I realized the presence of the cool and still night. Then I saw Mrs. Swoon crying, *"Operation Anaconda..."* Whoever gets to give these separate little missions names has a pretty cool role. "Hmm, what do you guys think we should call this one? Hey, let's name this one after a snake!" The whole situation was just so strange though. Ford, nor the affair at Denny's registered right, because it all seemed too unreal, set up - almost like it was a badly performed play with some underlying message. *Gates and Flames?* Though, that message was a little too much. *"I go outside myself and look at me... I look at myself, and about what I love. Why do you run?"* This last statement got me. *Why do I run?* I tried to leap outside of myself like Ford had told me. There I was, just running on the sidewalk. It was like when I was on morphine, and I could float away from my body. *I guess that I look at peace. Is running my purpose then? Surely not, I'm very slow compared to a lot of people.*

It was almost as if Ford Swoon had something to do with my newfound Godliness... I looked up to the dark stars scattered around the sky, their charisma amplified by the quietness. The peace of the night creates a sort of prism of beauty through which to see and hear things with a new clear perspective. I noticed a constellation that looked like an upside-down arch, a little lopsided at the sides. I thought about the butt-chinned man from *Heaven's Gates and Hell's Flames*, and then Daniel, the evangelical stranger. I then realized that both of them were spreading the absolute opposite of what I have found to be true Christianity. I found God because I felt alone and hopeless.

I found God because of a feeling I couldn't find elsewhere, but only in the deepest, darkest moments of my life... a feeling that shot through me, not physically, not even in a sudden enhancement of emotions, but a new spiritual world I felt a connection to beyond a normal mindset. This world was above and beyond my understanding, but for some reason my heart desired it so strongly that I held onto it. *Gates and Flames* pulled me into Christianity with a scare tactic. Daniel probably scares people. "Have you ever heard of a place called Hell, ma'am? Do you know what it means to repent?" No wonder so many people think Christianity is uncool, so ridiculous. No wonder people think Christians are uptight hypocrites.

This was just too wrong. I wanted to tell everyone that has ever been in the audience of *Heaven's Gates and Hell's Flames* that fear of hell is not why people are Christians. I wanted to explain to all of the victims of Daniel and people like him that perfection is not what Christianity is about, that it's about a connection to God through Jesus and the Holy Spirit… something that just comes into you and you can only experience yourself if you can open up to it.

I closed my eyes to let the fresh breeze cool my eyelids which were hot from all of my thinking. My legs were still moving, and I realized that I had forgotten about them. My spiritual moment of deep thought seemed to vanish suddenly, and I faced reality again. The night was the only thing around. I glanced from one direction to the next, and I recognized where I was. The trees were all behind me. To my surprise, tall buildings of brick and stone stood on either side of me. I had run all the way from my house on the north side of town, made a long circle around the residential area in the middle, to old downtown St. Joseph, which must have been at least 12 miles. I was amazed that I had not even paid attention to where I was going, or even how long I had been running. I don't think I'd ever thought about things so deeply before. The thoughts blinded me from my tired leg muscles, my racing heart, from reality. Stunned at my achievement, I looked around for a minute, breathing heavily.

19

Why do I Run?

Late Fall 2002

I was a senior in fall of 2002, and I was at the end of my last cross-country season ever. Coach always let's the seniors, if they haven't ran a varsity race before, run varsity for their last race of the season, the Conference Championships. At the time, Missouri was divided into four sections, eight districts, and sixteen conferences. Based on where your high school is located geographically, you are placed in a particular conference. There are eight cross-country teams in our conference. The conference championships are held at the end of each regular season, and the top three teams from that conference will move onto district championships, sectionals, and finally, the state championships.

There are, of course, multiple people running from one team in a single race, and there must be at least seven. Each runner scores individual points for their team based upon their placing in the finish chute. Only the first seven runners to finish from one team score points for their team. Say the first runner on a team gets 10th place in the race and the next runner comes in 20th place, that team would have scored 30 points thus far. This goes all the way up to the seventh runner from that team, who might come in at 50th place, thus adding 50 points to the team's final score. The team that comes out of the race with the lowest amount of points gets first place overall.

It was generally expected that the Central Cross-Country team (girls and boys) were most certainly going to win at conference, districts, and most likely go to state; a fine group of worthy competitors.

· · ·

2002 Missouri Suburban 8 Cross-Country Championships
November 2002
Smithville Lake, MO

I was chewing on a peanut butter Power Bar, the flavor of
champions. During each bus ride, I would calculate to start eating
the Power Bar exactly 45 minutes before the gun was to blow for
my race. I would take the bar with a six ounce cup of room
temperature water. Supposedly, this allows the body just the right
amount of moisture and time to completely absorb the wonders of
the bar, thus yielding the maximum power and resulting in the
best performance. Since the Conference Championships are the
last race for a lot of us, Coach lets all of the seniors run varsity if
they want to. I was going to do it. This was my first and last
varsity race, and I needed as much power as possible.

During my chewing and sipping, I glanced around the bus to see
if anyone else was as relaxed as I was. I actually had room to
move around and look at the other people in the bus this time
because I was a senior. This gave me the right to have a seat to
myself and have the extreme pleasure of yelling, "Freshmen and
sophomores double up!"

The bus arrived at our destination at the presumed time, and the
second I got out Coach called out in his monotone yell "Freshman
girls gun goes in 30 minutes. Jog the course, get stretched and
ready!" This gave us very little time to get ready for the race,
considering it is best to stretch for about 20 minutes, and it
usually takes 15 minutes to jog through enough of the course to
get a feel for it. The course for this race was a giant oblong circle.
The race consisted of two laps around the O, so we jogged one lap
quickly through the first half of the race. When we got back to
the tent that was still being set up by the rest of the team, Coach
Price was handing out numbered flags to pin on ourselves for the
race.

"Hey Johnny Hotpants... Pin this on your bad self." It was my
racer number on a piece of paper. It was 5065 I think. The

numbers seemed to always be in the thousands. I pinned the paper on my black jersey, which still had JHP sewn on the shoulder.

Varsity guys finish in 16 and 17 minutes. My best so far was 19:10, an average time for that year's junior varsity team.

The gun for the freshman girls went off, then the boys, then junior varsity. The gun for the varsity boys' race would be the last one to go. It was the final race… the main event - like at a boxing match where you see four or so other matches before the main one. There was still 20 minutes until my race, and to suppress my growing nervousness, I started chewing some grapes I carried in a baggie.

My family was approaching and waving at me from the bottom of a hill, even Kristin's little dog, Chance, followed along. Kristin and Casey had on these Relay For Life team shirts that a group of my friends made while I was in New York. Some people in school still wore them every once in a while. On the front in the upper right-hand corner was my name in bright blue lettering. On the back, was a big animated picture of a kid pulling his shorts halfway down and his butt. This was supposed to be a symbol for my hotpants. Over the years, someone had gotten the true story behind the name Hotpants mixed up with the pair of butt-shorts I wore a couple times. Underneath the picture of the kid with the butt was the phrase, "We're behind yah all the way!"

I was mentally preparing, trying to calm the butterflies in my stomach. The time went fast, and before I knew it, it was time to report down to the starting line to run my final race. Before I left, Coach Price held both my shoulders and gave me a few words of encouragement.

"Once you reach the point where you can't do anything else, to the end of what you can do, that's where faith begins. Johnny, you can do anything through Christ who gives you strength."

...

The breeze hit my face. It was quiet and peaceful inside my head. The intimidating and growling athletes were hopping around doing their form running, all in a graceful slow-motion dance. The white puffy clouds seemed to smile at me from far above like Care Bears. The rays of the sun shooting down between the groups of clouds covered me like a warm blanket. I slowly brought my hands up into my line of sight and experienced the peace of my open palm. The palm looked back at me like an innocent puppy dog. Then, with the swiftness, ease, and quietness of a ninja, the hand closed suddenly into a tight fist, all in a deep ceremonial vision, and I looked up.

Sucking in the vitality of the moment, I sung to myself in my head, *Eye of the Tiger*. I visualized myself as the eye. I leaped like a mean cat into form running, and I executed all of the motions with perfection. However, the runners all across the line were intimidating. I was one of the shortest competitors.

The five-minute gun hit the air with a blast. The team gathered about 20 meters away from the line to pray, to give blessing to the final race. We huddled up like a band of brothers. Justin was across from me, Curtis, Morton, Nathan, and Gilleland were all around me.

BAM!

A split second before the gun went off, the clouds, trees, grass suddenly seemed to implode into the gun, and freeze once everything was sucked in. Then as the gun popped, the entire world blasted back out in a fraction of the time it took to implode.

The entire place exploded, and the infamous funnel started closing in quickly. Our slot was unfortunately in the middle of the starting line. To my surprise, however, I was keeping up with everyone well. The rest of the guys were right in front of me. It was hard running, but the first 200 meters always were, so it seemed right. *If I just maintain this frame of mind, and make it a priority to stay right behind the other guys, then I should be just fine!*

As the enormous mass of runners hit the path, I spotted my family cheering from the midst of the ecstatic crowd. I had a huge smile on my face. I was thrilled that I was keeping up this well in my first varsity race. I stayed right behind the other six teammates.

In seconds, the mass morphed to the giant worm twisting and turning throughout the rough course. The Central group was running at about 50 meters back from the head of the worm that was about 150 meters in length. We were out in the open for the first quarter mile, and finally we all disappeared into a thicket of trees. My heart was already pumping hard. It had only been about 30 seconds, and the group of Central guys seemed a meter or two more ahead of me than before. I tried hard not to think about the pain, and I turned my attention to a bird high in one of the trees looking down at us, apparently being entertained by the race. It was a good looking red cardinal with bright, shiny black eyes. I tried to imagine the cardinal's point of view. It must have been kind of funny to watch so many humans running wildly like we were, all with these crazy expressions on our faces.

Once we were well past the cardinal, I kept a close eye on the increasingly rough terrain before me, paying attention to the detail in the ground. Then I started to think about what type of life might be living in each crevice on the ground, or what was going on in the many anthills I passed. *Perhaps it is a town gathering, a day off work to get front row seats for the race. Either that, or a declared state of emergency within the ant cities because the strongest of all earthquakes is crushing them over and over.*

The ants quickly disappeared from my head as we turned sharp corners through the trees, snapping sticks and leaves on the ground like a series of firecrackers. It was nearly a half mile into the race, and the worm had spread out a good deal. Runners from different teams were passing me at a moderate pace. Running varsity is no joke. Runners entered my peripheral vision about every ten seconds, and by the time they were ten feet in front of me, one or two more stepped in.

We were coming up on the first mile mark, about 200 meters out of the trees. There was a large crowd screaming all along the sidelines. It was easy to pick out my family. I smiled at them, but it was more a smirk underneath all of the stress in my legs and increasing pain in my chest as my heart slammed against it, pumping blood so hard it made my veins cringe, like when the nurses would pull too hard on the syringe. Standing around the mile mark, was a group of coaches, including Coach Price. "5:13... 14... 15!!!" he shouted out to each runner as they passed. He caught my eye and winked as I blew by like a strong gust of wind as he shouted "5:15!" It was the fastest mile I had ever run. This was actually very horrible. Everyone knows that it is death to PR the first mile in a 3.1-mile race. I usually ran about a 5:30 in a timed mile. That meant I should be running my first mile in around 6:15 in a race, no faster, or I would burn out way too soon. I had made a huge mistake trying to keep up with the regular varsity runners.

It had only been a mile and a quarter, and I was already feeling like I couldn't go on much farther. My chest felt broken. My leg muscles strained hard, and there was a painful tingling all over my body like the masquerade of a thousand bees within me. The time between each runner passing me increased from ten seconds to about five.

We were coming around back towards the starting line, completing our first lap. At least I was, who knew how far the head of the worm was. The thick crowd screamed even more as we passed. There were so many screams, but despite my impaired hearing, I could easily pick out the voices of my family, and I spotted them again. I must have been very far behind and looked miserable with the crinkles of pain and sweat flying off my face. Everyone in my family still cheered their hardest just as if I had been winning. Then I noticed my sister's dog again, Chance. He was smiling as well. He was enjoying the race like the cardinal was. It was then that I thought of Mr. Mischief. I wished that I was back at the mansion on Lover's Lane, taking a nap on the red couch in the little TV room, resting my head on Mr. Mischief like a pillow. I could almost feel the warmth of his fur and the up-and-down movement of his breathing against my cheek.

It was about the time that I ran underneath the cover of trees for the second time, that I realized the pain was overwhelming. My run had turned into a fast, desperate hobble. I looked behind and saw a group of runners closing in on me, so it was all I could do to speed up again. This gave me some hope though, because I knew that I was not yet in dead last.

I popped out of the trees at a quickened pace, refusing to be passed again. However, the other runners were right on my tail and my energy reserves were at zero, just like my blood counts a year before. I was still running and puffing as hard as I could, but I must have been slowing down because two runners passed by. The exit from the trees was at the top of a hill, and from it you could see the entire rest of the course. I could see the rest of the long worm as it progressed farther and farther through the hills, which lasted a little over a mile, and then came back around over a few steep, and almost rocky hills to finally end at the finish chute.

To my surprise, the head of the worm wasn't *that* far away. I had run my first mile very well, which put me at a good place. It was only after a mile and a half into the race that my strength quickly dwindled. There were exactly 1.1 miles left in the race because I had just passed the 2-mile mark. *If I just stick it out, it will be all over soon. I might still have a chance of getting a decent place... Ah! Who am I kidding? I am practically dead.* As the head of the worm was making its way up the final hill before the turn around, I spotted the group of regular varsity guys. They were still running together. Although a little spread out, they all had to be within three or four arm lengths of each other.

My thinking must have slowed me even more because two other runners passed me. Again I tried to make myself accelerate forward with an explosion of energy that wasn't there. My body simply couldn't do it. The sweat rolled off me so fast that it seemed to fall and wet my shoes, because I thought I felt a sloshing sound with every pounding step. I could see that my arms were dangling on either side of me, flopping in the wind like cans behind a just-married car.

The consequences of giving up were unbearable, but I was simply at the end. I was too beaten to think and realize the pain of my face hitting the rough ground and skidding to a stop. I didn't even

215

feel my knees and elbows scraping across the dirt, but as much as I tried, as much as I wanted it, as much as I wanted to avenge all that was ever taken away from me, all I could tell myself was, *I'm no hero. Look at me...* I looked behind to see if there were still any runners behind me, about to trample over me... only to see my racing number lying on the ground, half ripped up by the fall, about to blow away in the wind...

My next move did not seem to help me out at all or even infuse in me some hidden strength or even from the Heavens, because I just closed my eyes and prayed. I didn't pray that God would teleport me 10 meters from the finish line. I didn't pray for God to make Mr. Mischief and our red couch appear. I didn't even pray for God to make it all stop, as one might think that would be the proper prayer at that drastic time, but I prayed for God to simply take me away – to just lift from my body the pain and humiliation of falling, so I wouldn't have to feel it anymore. I had given up like a pitiful fool; lying in the dirt and begging for mercy. I was numb from pain and I didn't feel Him as He lifted me away, but I could feel a cold and refreshing breeze on my face, as if it were His breath.

It was then that I opened up my eyes, unaware that they had been closed. I found myself still running and puffing like a steam engine at full throttle. My fall had just been an awful illusion, a strong vision. Such intense exhaustion can do that to you. It took me a second to shake off the shock of being back in reality, and I glanced behind me. I did not only see the two runners that had passed me just after the trees, still struggling over the last hill before the turn, but I saw all of the hills, and very far off at the end of them, the thicket of trees from which I had come. I turned back and slowly but surely, the extreme roaring crowd gathering on either side of the glorious finish chute materialized at the far corner of my sight. I was turning the final corner and closing in on the finish line. The finish chute gleamed like Dorothy's first sight of the City of Oz. I could see that the rest of the Central runners were just crossing the finish line. Not being able to talk, having no reason to say anything, and nobody around to say it to - I was speechless.

Perhaps I exceeded the limits of my conscious mind, and I had been lost in a sort of lucid day dream. I had been praying, and I was lost in my prayer. It didn't go away, but all physical strain went out of focus. My body was still struggling and beating itself, but my mind and heart were somewhere else. I was still the mediocre runner in my own shoes, but God was my wing.

That moment became the foundation of my life and the core of my Christianity. That moment is tattooed on my shoulder. I wish everyone could experience this whoever they are, and wherever they are in their lives. Whatever they believe, whoever thinks God is stupid, empty, or made-up... I wish they would think twice, not by having someone shove salvation down their throat, or by fear of hell, but by finding and experiencing this incredible feeling for themselves, at their own level.

The Holy Spirit is real, and it moves in this life, and it can be experienced.

The roar of the crowd pierced my feeble ears. The ringing rang louder than ever, but I was still in a state of prayer, and it was still OK. I could see that all of my team had made it in already. I could also see my family and my sister's dog Chance cheering like crazy within the masses of people. I smiled a very big smile.

I finished at 105th place and collapsed into Mom at the end of the chute. My teammates had kicked in towards the end, being the varsity runners they were, and had all taken places within the top fifteen, including first. I was the 12th runner to make it in for the Central varsity team, and I didn't add to the score of the first seven runners. Central took 1st place at the 2002 Conference Championships and went on to win at districts, sectionals, and they placed 4th at State.

20
A MISSION

May, 2003

I returned home to my bed and to an aging Mr. Mischief. Mr. Mischief would not live for the rest of my senior year of high school. In fact it was only a week or two before school let out that news of his passing had hit the hearts of everyone in town. On the day after his death, there was a tribute to Mr. Mischief over the video announcements at Central High School: a slow zoom into a photo of him laying down curled up and looking straight into the camera.

Everything back at school was the same. I wore my hearing aids every day. People who didn't know me wondered, and little kids stared, but eventually, I didn't even think about them. Hearing aids made me hear, and that was all I needed. The ringing in my ears has never stopped. It rings that glorious sound in my ears even as I write these words. But I like to think of it, every time I notice it, as a reminder of everything that had happened, a sort of battle scar.

It didn't take long to see that my life was much more meaningful than it would have been if cancer had never happened. Although I was miserable during that time, and there are countless side effects that will haunt me for the rest of my life, I am glad about what had happened to me. Without it, I would not have experienced Cider House Rules. I wouldn't have made a home in Memphis or New York City. I wouldn't have the same love for life that I do now. I don't think that my family would have been as close as it is now if it weren't for cancer, St. Jude's, The Ronald McDonald House, or for Memorial Sloan Kettering.

The best thing that came out of my experiences with cancer, was that I found myself spiritually, and learned what Christianity *really* means.

So at home, I started eating cereal again. I remained friends with Jerry and we would make frequent trips to Denny's late at night. I never saw or heard of Ford Swoon's mom again, but I will

218

always remember Ford Swoon, the strange kid that taught me why life was worth living. He glorified his life by joining the army and dying for what he loved to do. It was his purpose. In that sense, I think I discovered my purpose as well. *Cider House Rules* instilled this love in me. Making movies and storytelling is a passion of mine, and in a lot of ways, I totally believe it's my purpose.

Memphis will always hold a large piece of my heart. For two years after the day I walked out, I went back to Memphis with my family every three months for checkups and MRI's to make sure I was still cancer-free. After two years was up, I went every six months for a year. And now I only go once a year, and still no sign of cancer. Currently, it has been nearly five and a half years since I left cancer behind. I am satisfied that I have successfully destroyed it forever, and avenged myself many times over. Life randomly goes up, down, and sideways every day. That's what's cool right? Life situations are going to happen, good and bad. But you shouldn't let life deprive you of living.

Every time I go back to St. Jude's, I see children coming with their families for the first time. I look at them and feel a wave of pity, for I know what journeys they are about to embark on. But I only look at them and smile like a veteran cancer patient should, just like those old people that would stare at me through the windows of their rooms when I first came to the St. Joseph hospital. However, this is a good look. It is a smile that says, "I know - It is stupid to tell you not to be afraid. It's good to be nervous and afraid sometimes, to get your heart pumping before the race. A great foe lies before you. Keep heart, stay tough, don't only rely on worldly strength alone. When you come out on the other side, no matter how long it seems, even years after you leave this place, you'll find that you are ten times the person you were before, and you will do great things." What is really cool, is that sometimes the kids seem to understand everything and smile back at me.

Every time I go back, I see Dr. Gajjar and run into old nurses that still know my name. None of the people have changed at St. Jude's since I had been there. There have been new doctors, nurses, and new paint jobs, but the heart of the place is always

the same. It will always be one of the best places in the world…
not because it is filled with sad cancer-fighting kids, but because
St. Jude's saves the lives of innocent children from all over the
world every day, and it makes them better people.

Also, St. Jude's does change all the time. They are constantly
researching new, more efficient ways to fight pediatric cancer.
They are constantly getting better at leaving less and less side
effects in the children they treat. Every time I go, there are new
physical improvements to the hospital, such as new buildings,
new departments, new colors, and new artwork from children.
Though, every time I walk to the D Clinic waiting room, I'll
always visualize one painting in particular with angels.

Sadly though, I don't think I ever settled into the state I so much
desired throughout my life. I have never become normal. I never
was satisfied that I successfully blended in with the crowd. I have
never succumbed to the stereotypical ways of mainstream society
enough to earn the badge of a "general person." After my junior
year of high school, I began to learn the mere absurdity of my
jealousy.

What is normal?

I'm not really sure what normal is, but I have come to the theory
that life is not meant to be normal, it's just meant to be worth it.

I enjoyed every minute of the rest of high school. I had finally
made it to the end - the end of the first part of the journey.
Beyond that, my dream was to be a storyteller, and a filmmaker.

The search for a good film school is a challenge itself. It's tough
to decide whether to go out west and pay 60 grand to get caught
in a mess of wanna-be producers and directors - drown amongst
a giant pool of talent, but be guaranteed a PA job on a studio
backed feature when you graduate… or go to a smaller school
with more individual attention, much more hands-on
accessibility, an opportunity to let your talent develop, but be
dropped out into the immense, unpromising, and unmerciful
world of independent filmmakers and freelancers after
graduation.

I didn't want to work to be the bottom of someone else's big. I wanted to be the top of my small. So I enrolled in a small, but reputable film school in St. Louis, Missouri: the world headquarters of Webster University.

My mission is to entertain, to inspire, and to witness to a mass audience, glorifying God and Christianity based on the way I experienced it, not out of a blind fear of Hell.

My mission is to get my story out, to lift up the spirit of my cat, lift up people that are different, glorify distance running, and unveil the joys of breakfast cereal. My mission is to share my story and other people's stories like it.

This is my movie; waiting to be made. Therefore, I have to take it step by step, working towards my goal each day. I knew that the first thing I needed to do, in order to one day make my movie, was to write it all down.

Johnny Cathcart lives in New York working as a
documentary filmmaker.
He is constantly seeking to tell other people's
unique stories of overcoming life-changing trials.
He is still writing, and still running.

Acknowledgments: The greatest inspiration for this book has been my amazing family: Mom, Dad, Kristin, and Casey. They've been a fantastic support through my cancer journey and beyond. I want to thank my friends who stuck with me all the way. Thank you to my unofficial editors, Erin Duley, Nicole Wolfe, Danielle Dorsey, Diane Byers, and my mom. The Central Cross Country Team has been amazing to me. This book would not exist if it weren't for the extraordinary love they showed. Thank you Coach O'Brien and Coach Price for encouraging me to be resilient in the face of adversity. Thank you to my friends and extended family for all of your prayers and support. My greatest thanks goes to Jesus, the living savior, redeemer, and the daily motivator of my life.

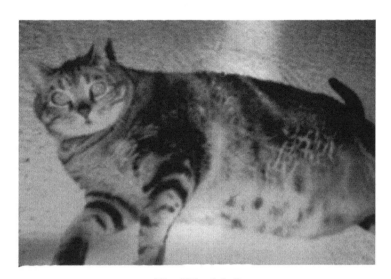

Mr. Mischief

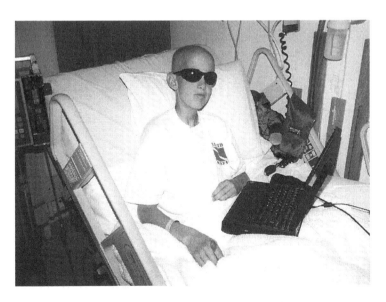

Chilling at Hospital in Memphis

Mom and Kristin in NYC

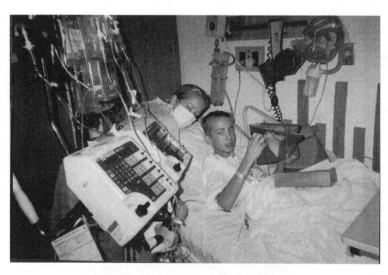

Mom and I at Hospital in NYC

**Me (in hat) and the team at MO State CC Championships,
with white JHP patch on their shoulders**

Coach O'Brien and I

Brian Prashak and I in NYC

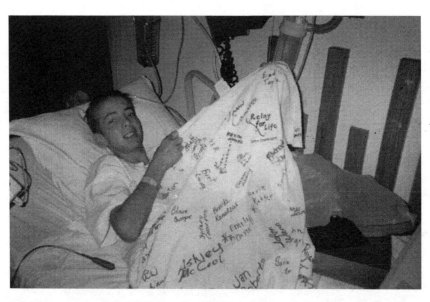

Holding up a big T-shirt that friends made and sent to NYC

**Toby Maguire and I holding
Cider House Rules clap board**

**Dressed up as an orphan on set the Cider House Rules,
being rabbit-eared by Kieran Culkin**

Made in the USA
Charleston, SC
31 October 2015